Supporting
Writing

Supporting Writing

Sylvia Edwards

Series edited by Sylvia Edwards and Angela Wilson

 David Fulton Publishers

David Fulton Publishers Ltd
The Chiswick Centre, 414 Chiswick High Road, London W4 5TF

www.fultonpublishers.co.uk

First published in Great Britain in 2004 by David Fulton Publishers.

10 9 8 7 6 5 4 3 2 1

Note: The right of Sylvia Edwards to be identified as the author of this work has been asserted by her in accordance with the Copyright, Designs and Patents Act 1988.

Copyright © Sylvia Edwards 2004

British Library Cataloguing in Publication Data
A catalogue record for this book is available from the British Library.

David Fulton Publishers is a division of Granada Learning, part of ITV plc.

ISBN 1 84312 209 X

Typeset by FiSH Books
Printed and bound in Great Britain

Contents

Introduction

Supporting Writing is aimed at teaching assistants, but will be welcomed by all staff involved in teaching children how to write. The book guides readers through the developmental process of becoming a writer. It provides a wealth of information on how children learn to write alongside practical strategies and resources for supporting writing.

The remodelling of the school workforce heralds significant change for all schools as teaching assistants are assigned greater responsibilities. This book aims to help teaching assistants, whatever their level of experience, to support the development of writing independently. It also reflects the requirements of the National Curriculum and the National Literacy Strategy (NLS) (now part of the Primary Strategy) as the driving forces behind the writing curriculum in most schools.

A companion title to *Supporting Spelling* also in this series – both areas of learning must go hand in hand for writing to develop – *Supporting Writing* focuses on learning to write in Key Stages 1 and 2 with the major emphasis on writing in Key Stage 1. At this stage, the basic foundations must be laid if learners are to achieve success through later key stages. Staff in secondary schools may find this book valuable as a resource for helping writers in Key Stage 3 who have not yet reached the age-expected attainment in writing.

Although not intended to cover special educational needs, brief references have been made where relevant to the issue under discussion. Staff in special schools will also find this book helpful.

I hope you enjoy the book and find it inspiring and useful to your support role.

Chapter 1

'Independent writing': what do we mean?

This chapter explores what we mean by independent writing and considers the 'what, why and who' of writing as communication.

What is a writer?

You are a writer! We are all writers in the broadest sense. While only a minority of adults turn to writing as a profession, as adults we compose a significant amount of written material during the course of a typical week or month.

So, while you may not have written a novel (yet), what have you written? Make a list of everything (for both home and work) – you may surprise yourself. My own list included:

- List of things to do (I'm a prolific list-maker).
- List of items needed from the garden centre.
- This chapter.
- Note to my daughter.
- Amendments to a policy for work.
- Letter to a friend (I'm not into text messaging yet!).
- Report on a pupil.
- Shopping list.
- Diary entries (dates and meetings – not the Anne Frank type).

This is only part of my list, but enough to show the variations. Your list may be similar. Over the course of a month you may have composed writing in a range of **formats**, for example, lists, prose, diagrams, charts, poetry and flow diagrams. Most of this writing is likely to have been **non-fiction** but may have included **fiction** if you write novels or stories.

What do we write about?

Writing is about *life*, whether it is a letter to a relative, a note to the milkman, a job application or a list of what to get friends and family for Christmas. If we each were to put samples of our writing into a plastic bag and bury it in the garden, what a wonderful picture of life in the 21st century would eventually be communicated to future generations (if found). Writing through the ages bears out this fact. We know about history through the writers of the time. And we have only to read letters from soldiers during World War I to appreciate the potential power of writing, especially when it communicates from the heart.

Why do we write?

Think about the purposes for your own writing. If you wrote a list of some kind was it a memory aid? Perhaps you wrote a text message to arrange a time to meet. Or maybe you wrote a report on a child for an **individual education plan (IEP) review** meeting. Consider the reader whose list included a job application. The purpose of this would be to persuade a potential employer of his/her suitability for the post. The purpose for writing anything determines how we write it. We may write to persuade, to record, to recount an event, to explain, to apologise, to report, to inform, to question or to instruct (more on text types in Chapter 6).

Why do children need to learn to write? If a child asked you this question how would you answer? Many children don't see the point of writing. Some switch off as soon as they realise they cannot cope; others groan at the very idea of writing and fail to enjoy the experience, even if they are high achievers. Children need to know *why* and for what *purpose* they are learning to write. This knowledge will help to fire the enthusiasm of most learners.

Who do we write for?

Sometimes writing is for us – a diary or shopping list – but other forms of writing may be for others to read. Consider your own writing again. Did you write a diary (Anne Frank style), committing your thoughts and feelings onto paper for yourself? That report on a pupil – was it for the special educational needs co-ordinator (SENCO), the parent, the child himself or other involved staff? Did you write a letter to accompany some flowers sent to a friend in hospital?

Who we write for is as important as why we write as this determines the tone of the text. Your personal diary entries can be as untidy as you like. The note to your friend in hospital needs to be readable, comforting and informally warm – you may even end the note with kisses. Conversely, a report on a child is one of the formal pieces of writing required of staff in schools. A letter to the head teacher of your child's school will be written in a different tone than one sent to a friend.

Audience is an important factor when we are thinking about writing.

Writing as part of language and literacy

Writing is part of literacy. Literacy is defined as being able to read and write. But what is the relationship between writing and the other components of literacy and language?

All writing involves spelling. How far does achievement in writing depend on good spelling? Poor spellers often end up as 'switched-off' writers as the 'stops and starts' of struggling to spell inhibit writing flow. Although writing is inextricably linked with spelling, we need to consider each set of skills separately in order to teach and support them together (see *Supporting Spelling* in this series). For the purpose of this book, writing refers to the combining of words into sentences and text according to the linguistic conventions of English. The NLS structures the teaching objectives at word, sentence and text levels: spelling is at word level while writing is at sentence and text levels.

How is writing linked with reading? Are good readers generally good writers? Good writers depend upon reading in many ways. For a start, reading offers us models of good writing. How can we write a novel if we have never read one? How do we know what a list looks like if we have never seen one? How can we write an article for a magazine if we have never studied the structure? How can we write a letter of complaint if we have not seen examples of such letters and the type of language used?

What exactly do we take from reading to support our writing (and spelling)? At word, sentence and text levels, reading provides us with a range of language that we model for writing. **Grammar** and **syntax** are integral parts of this language structure and without examples we cannot produce them in writing. Reading offers the language experience from which writing develops. All writers write from their experiences of life and bring to the writing process their knowledge of spoken language. This brings us to the link between speaking and listening.

Think about what happens when we talk. Subconsciously the rules and conventions of language that you have grown up with are brought into play according to the purpose for speaking and the audience to whom you are speaking. Start by completing each of the following sentences with a *single* word that makes sense:

> Please can we go to the ... ?
> He ran ... to catch the train.
> She was wearing a lovely, ... coat.
> The dog was sitting ... the table.

For the first sentence I inserted *shop/supermarket/park*. Perhaps you noticed that the first set of *single* words would need to be **nouns**. What did you insert for the second one? In all probability it was an **adverb** – *quickly/hurriedly/anxiously*. For the third sentence you probably used an **adjective** to describe the coat further. For the last example you may have thought of *under/beside/on*, all of which are **prepositions**.

Now think about the following **verb patterns**:

| run | ran | have run | am running | had run | would have run |
| eat | ate | have eaten | am eating | had eaten | would have eaten |

Of course, these are all different tense structures that can be created from the two verbs – to run and to eat.

Finally, think about the different forms of the same root word:

intend	intended	intending	intention
review	reviewed	reviewing	review

Which form of each word would you place in the gaps?

It had been my . . . to . . . that policy, but I didn't have time.

You may have inserted *intention* in the first gap and *review* in the second. But how did you know which form of each word to choose? Without a sound knowledge of grammar we would not be able to compose sentences as we would have no idea of how words go together to make sense. We would not dream of asking the following question: *Would like some you cream ice?* Our knowledge of **word class** (noun, adjective, verb etc.) and **word form** (intend or intended?), as well as the sequence of words, governs writing composition.

The dreaded 'grammar' word may bring back memories for some people of boring and meaningless exercises. Yet, writing depends on knowledge about grammar and can cause considerable difficulties for some children who do not possess this knowledge. In order to master writing, we must have mastered grammar through talk. Some practical suggestions for work on grammar are included in Chapter 4.

Writing composition

This is NLS speak for the act of putting words and sentences together to form **text**. Consider how a composer puts notes together to make music. Good writing is like beautiful music and this book looks at how children can become composers of writing that has the impact, as well as the rhythms and beats, of a musical score.

Writing today!

We only have to read the letters written by Jane Austen or Dickens to imagine the changes between their time and ours. Even the last few years have made a huge difference to how our generation views writing. First, the rules and conventions of grammar that many of us were taught at school have become considerably relaxed. I was taught never to start a sentence with the words *because/and/but*, yet you will find numerous examples in this book, and writing in general, to illustrate the grammatical 'laxity' of writing today. The concept of writing in 2004 is nothing like that of our grandparents or even our parents.

Consider the text message. I struggle to send one as I really cannot get to grips with this 'short-cut' way of composing writing. Yet, younger people send numerous text messages every day and in a fraction of the time it must have taken Jane Austen to write her letters.

What else has changed? ICT has made a huge impact on the way in which most of us communicate. I am just about getting to grips with emails although I am probably far less comfortable with this style of writing than the majority of people. Consider how the Internet has opened up opportunities for writing. How we teach and support writing today must reflect the learners of today if they are to appreciate the point of writing. But therein lies the dilemma – how do we encourage children to learn to spell and to write according to the rules and conventions when these are fast becoming a distant memory for many children, with possibly fewer models of conventional writing for them to observe?

What about handwriting? What should we say to children who protest that good handwriting no longer matters as they can use the computer or their mobile? The tension between handwriting skills and 'writing today' presents educators with a considerable problem. How strongly should we push neat handwriting and letter formation, especially for those children who struggle with this skill, when we could offer them a laptop? (See later for more on handwriting.)

There are no set answers, but these issues carry implications for how we approach writing in schools. Many children write through ICT using text messaging, emails and the Internet with amazing ease. The way we teach and support writing and the resources we use must reflect the writing of today if children are to enjoy their writing and become writers.

Writing as communication

The previous section focused on writing today and the different ways in which we communicate through writing. Whatever tools we use, the main point of writing is to communicate a message. Good writers write like readers! They have empathy and adjust their message accordingly. So being able to match the tone, style and formality in accordance with the purpose of the message and the reader (audience) is what we are aiming towards.

Writing can be permanent. When we write we create meaning in a way that cannot be retrieved. Once said, speech at least can be forgotten over time and harsh words can be eclipsed from the memory. Conversely, the written word cannot be taken back. We place our hearts and minds on the line for others to see and sometimes to judge. We are encouraged to place our feelings, opinions, needs and desires on paper. Therefore, if we want children to use writing sensitively and skilfully as a communicative device, then we must also be sensitive when responding to what they have written.

Summary

In this chapter I have looked at:

- Writing as a reflection of life.
- What we write – in a range of formats.
- Why we write – purpose.
- Who we write for – audience.
- Writing as part of literacy and language.
- Writers as 'word composers'.
- Writing in our modern world.
- Writing as communication.

The following chapter considers some important principles for those who support writing.

Chapter 2

Principles for supporting writing

Teaching children how to write has many pitfalls. This chapter outlines some principles that may help to avoid those pitfalls so that all children can progress as writers.

Inclusion

The National Curriculum inclusion statements (DfEE/QCA 1999) underpin teaching and learning. Consider how these apply to our support of writing:

1. *Removing barriers to learning.* This statement is to do with *all* children having access to the curriculum, in this context the writing curriculum. Children with physical difficulties need special consideration with regard to where they sit in class. Children with sensory difficulties may need special equipment to enable them to engage. Other types of barriers, often emotional, may be less obvious. If a child *feels* that he/she cannot 'do' a particular task, then this is a barrier to learning. We all know the 'I can't do it' scenario. Problems such as lack of adequate spoken language, poor spelling and lack of motivation can all act as barriers to success in writing.

2. *Setting suitable challenges* for all learners. Most of life is a challenge in one form or another. In this context we are concerned with the challenges for children that are represented as objectives and targets. Challenges for learner writers may be to *use adjectives in sentences* or to *write simple sentences, each with words in sequence and a full stop.* All challenges need to be realistic so that the learner can rise to that

particular challenge and achieve the objectives. If too easy, learning will hardly progress – if too difficult, they may become barriers that imply 'I can't' rather than 'I can'. Challenges for writing must enable success.

3. The third strand of the inclusion statement concerns *diversity*. Most classrooms contain a diverse range of learners with different cultural backgrounds, interests and learning styles.

Differentiation is encapsulated within the three inclusion statements outlined above. Some ideas for differentiation are incorporated into the content of further chapters.

Having the confidence to write

If children are to achieve in writing, they must have the confidence to attempt tasks set. This is where the idea of suitable challenges fits in. If the challenge seems achievable and the pupil glimpses success on the horizon, then confidence is high and he/she will 'have a go'. Confidence has a lot to do with self-esteem.

The current emphasis on emotional literacy is based on the premise that learning depends upon children's emotional well-being. Diversity takes account of how children learn. A report on the Foundation Stage (ATL 2004) stated that 'more emphasis should be given to sustained, purposeful talk, complex, imaginative play (as part of a) curriculum based on what we know about children and the ways in which they learn'. Children's confidence to attempt writing tasks stems from the perception that they can succeed.

Enjoyment and motivation

Learning to write can be extremely difficult for many children. It can also be boring if the activities do not take into account the range of interests and learning styles. So children must enjoy writing otherwise motivation stands no chance. Enjoyment also stems from confidence and learners' anticipation of success.

Real writing (purpose)

Who do children write for? Do they write for the adults who direct their writing activities or do they write for a real readership? By real, I mean people who will read what they have written as *readers*. Much writing in schools is done only to demonstrate that children can do it. Much of the time this is inevitable as schools have to reinforce the NLS objectives and there is a packed programme to get through.

If we want to motivate children to write with enthusiasm, then some of the writing done in school must be purposeful. For example, writing labels for the classroom cupboards, writing notices and instructions on walls, or writing stories for younger children in the school to enjoy. If the writing displayed around school lacks some of the neatness and correctness of that done by an adult, does it really matter as long as the piece does what it is supposed to do – communicate?

Process before product

Becoming an accomplished writer is a long and laborious process. As part of that process, from the accumulated pieces of written work there will be hundreds of crossings out, amendments, additions and deletions along the road to final accomplishment. If only some of this 'process' writing could be upfront and on centre stage rather than behind the scenes. Sadly, few examples of process drafts end up on display for parents' evenings. Yet, paying due attention to the process as well as the product can be a wonderful motivator for learners. The message that writing has to go through a process before it reaches the final draft is a number one principle that all children should understand. Many (especially those with learning difficulties) will breathe a sigh of relief as they realise that writing is not something they are expected to get right the first time round. We might ask ourselves if the redrafted piece with its crossings out and amended vocabulary is worth demonstrating as good practice for developing writers. If so much hard graft has gone into it, shouldn't we make an effort to appreciate the work? Children also need to be reminded that 'real' (professional) writers may work their way through numerous redrafts before they arrive at the final version. We need to show learners that we value the process pieces of writing just as much as the finished products.

Skill acquisition and sequence

Place yourself in the position of a beginner, learning a foreign language or how to paint. You would expect to learn your craft slowly, to build new learning onto previously acquired learning. Writing is also a craft that has to be learned in sequence.

While I am not suggesting that teaching something new must always wait until a previous objective has been achieved – that would be a long wait for some children – trying to teach new skills that rely on previous learning before that learning has been secured can cause much confusion. And confusion is the last thing we want if the aim is to encourage motivation. For example, we would not expect children to write complex sentences if they are still struggling to form simple ones. We would not teach commas before children have mastered full stops. At text level, we would not teach aspects of grammar for writing without ensuring that those same grammatical elements are used in speech.

Writing across the curriculum

Where does writing happen? Where do writers write? Everywhere. Children often fail to appreciate this fact. They appear to think that writing only happens in the writing lesson, as part of the literacy hour. Think about the writing done in science or history. How is this different to that in English? In science, children may write up the results of an experiment. In history, they may write about the invention of the telephone. In geography, children may design a chart to show different climate patterns.

This emphasises the importance of cross-curricular writing. When you compiled a list of your own writing, you were reminded that a huge proportion is presented in a format other than prose. The range of adult writing includes poetry, charts, bar charts and other graphs, flow diagrams and matrices. Words may be hidden among a bewildering array of lines, dots, dashes, circles and so on (diagrammatic format is briefly explored as part of non-fiction writing in Chapter 6). Cross-curricular writing reflects the range that children need to experience in order to prepare them for writing in the adult world.

Independence

The focus of this book is on independent writing. By this is meant the ability to compose sentences and larger texts. How can teaching assistants support the development of independent writing? Consider the following as starting points:

● Never do for a child what he can do for himself.

● Never complete a piece of writing for a child.

● Try not to help where help is not needed, but be on hand immediately it is required.

● Encourage the child to 'think' about writing.

● Provide aids that contribute to independence, for example, a **writing frame** (see Chapter 7).

● Try not to ask the child to copy unless absolutely necessary.

These are just some ways in which adults can promote independence in learners, but I am sure you can think of many more. Independence in writing is not simply a matter of whether or not an adult or other child is supporting the writing; independence stems from within the learner having been nurtured from the start of schooling and is closely linked with choice and decision-making.

The completion habit

As a general rule, writing activities should aim towards finished products. Occasionally, writing in the literacy hour will feature practice sessions in which the focus is on specific parts of a text – for example focused work on story beginnings – but for most purposes, children need to see an end result. We are all aware of children who over time accumulate a mass of half-finished work. Why is this? Many children simply write too slowly – they plod on, but run out of time. For some, spelling gets in the way and inhibits the thinking process while others struggle to dredge up ideas and suddenly find the time has gone. The reasons are varied, but the consequences can be potentially damaging to the way in which children perceive writing (and learning in general).

First, imagine how we may feel as adults if we write half a letter and then never finish it, or part of the shopping list and only get half the shopping. Perhaps we only get to read half of a gripping story and miss out on the ending. It is human nature to want to finish tasks and get that sense of satisfaction and pride from having done so. Some people are natural 'completer-finishers'.

Secondly, even if some children appear 'not bothered' about finishing pieces of writing, there is the issue of how we are preparing young people for adult life and the characteristics they carry into maturity. The ability to complete work as an adult, to see a project (often long-term) through to its end and to get a result stems from having done that regularly as part of the learning process. It involves self-discipline, independence and being able to sustain concentration and interest. I believe that children who regularly fail to complete writing tasks are at risk of developing what we might call the 'non-completion' habit. And 'non-completion' is not a healthy approach to adult life.

Thirdly, how are children to develop their skills and knowledge of writing if they end up with half-finished pieces? Would we leave a model of a Roman villa without its roof? This may seem an odd example but I hope it makes the point. The idea is unthinkable as children's perceptions of what a Roman villa looked like would be somewhat distorted, nor would we want a 'roofless' model on display in the classroom. Yet, we often leave pieces of writing 'without their roofs'.

So, although schools have to reflect the full range of writing, it seems to me that fewer completed pieces are preferable to many unfinished ones. If some children simply cannot complete all of the work required in the time available, what should we do? Should we aim for fewer pieces but focus more on quality? Should we allow time to complete work later in the week? The principle, if we want to encourage children to complete work, is that fewer pieces of quality writing are preferable to many pieces of unpolished or unfinished ones of which no one can be proud.

Writing as thought

At text level, as much time should be devoted to thinking as to putting words on paper (or keyboard). Unfortunately, children rarely consider

drama.

that there is a need to think about writing before it becomes a written piece. We all know those children who, once they have a pencil in their hand, start to write without any idea of where their writing is going. They may write a few words then sit back and wonder how to finish the sentence or they may get a few sentences down on paper, but ramble on with numerous 'ands' until the sequence is completely lost. Others get bogged down with dialogue, the 'he said' and 'she said' syndrome, all of which slows the pace of the writing and takes the content nowhere.

Children need to know that some writing has to be planned and strategies to help are included in Chapter 7.

■ Don't let spelling get in the way!

While the relationships between writing and other elements of literacy and language were mentioned in the previous chapter, the special relationship between writing and spelling merits greater attention. The aim, of course, is not to let spelling get in the way of writing progress. But this is easier said than done. Spelling is there. As golden thread, woven through the fabric of writing, it sparkles, magnetising the red pen. The problem is that spelling errors deflect attention from the writing itself. Strategies to encourage children not to let spelling get in the way could include:

● When responding to text level writing, comment first on the writing objectives. These may be to do with punctuation, sentence structure or story 'hooks'.

● Making it clear to children how you are going to respond to the writing before they start – and that spelling is not a high priority at this time.

● Encouraging 'have-a-go' approaches to spelling new words and trying not to let spelling interfere with thinking and composition.

● Trying not to 'give' children spellings in order to ease their spelling difficulties as this inhibits the 'have-a-go' habit that we wish to nurture and does nothing to develop spelling skills.

Balancing parts and wholes

Many prominent authors of children's books have recently campaigned to bring back 'real books'. They make the point that the NLS approach to literacy does not promote children's enjoyment as it overemphasises parts of texts in order to teach the objectives. Consequently, children are not enjoying literature as much as they did in the past.

So are children gradually being taught that they have to study everything they read, and that reading and writing cannot simply be enjoyed? I sincerely hope not. Balance is the key! If children do not study the parts with the wholes of texts, then how are they to learn how each part contributes to the finished writing? Whenever some part of a text is being worked on, always place it in the context of the whole piece so that children can see where the part belongs.

Developing healthy approaches to the perception of writing

Children's perceptions of writing start from their first experiences. The writing they see around them, the tasks they are asked to do and responses to their efforts all influence how children think about writing. So all of the principles above are important to how children perceive writing, which in turn influences how they become accomplished writers.

You may well have identified other principles for teaching writing, in which case I hope that the points I have made are compatible with yours and that this chapter has stimulated your thinking about the importance of teaching writing from the heart, with due regard to the learning outcomes. If we disregard what we know as principles of good practice, school writing experiences could end up as a mechanistic following of NLS objectives based around a dry and unappetising diet of routine and repetitive writing tasks, all of which will do nothing to inspire children or adults.

Summary

In this chapter I have looked at:

- The three strands of the National Curriculum inclusion statement.
- A number of important principles for teaching writing, all of which should help to ensure success for all learners at their own level.

drama

Chapter 3

Developing early writing

This chapter aims to raise your awareness of 'early writing', sometimes called 'emergent writing'. It features:

- The stages of development within early writing.
- Examples of early writing.
- Strategies and suggestions for developing early writing.
- Samples from the NLS objectives for writing at the early stages.
- A summary of National Curriculum Level 1 and the P scales for measuring small steps of progress.

What is early writing?

To answer the above question we need to ask at what point the act of putting pencil to paper actually becomes 'writing' and to what extent a child's first scribbles can be called writing. A child's initial attempts are often called **emergent writing,** as these represent the stage during which scribble and mark-making emerge into something that actually begins to look like writing that can communicate.

Gorman and Brooks (1996) identified seven stages of development in early writing. Stage 1 is that of drawing and sign writing, during which a child may have no idea what the writing 'says', but knows the difference between pictures and words. Such attempts appear to us as scribbles and shapes that have little meaning as writing.

Throughout stages 2, 3 and 4, this early writing becomes more like English script as the scribbles and shapes start to resemble letters. Even at this stage, the letters are not yet grouped into attempted words, but by stage 4, children have grasped the fundamental idea that writing is meant to communicate meaning even though the result is unrecognisable and the attempt at 'writing' cannot be deciphered independently by an adult.

By stage 5, children have begun to link the sounds and groups of letters with spoken words. They are now 'hearing' words more clearly, discriminating between the sounds and trying to link them to their attempts at spelling. This is the start of a long and complex journey involving **phonological awareness**. At this stage, we will start to see the first letters in words correctly placed, or a **dominant sound** in a word may appear within the mass of letters. The identification of sounds and the attempts at matching these to letters may still be random rather than strategic, as the child will not yet be placing the sounds in sequential order. Beyond stage 5, children begin to express concepts through their writing and set off along their personal developmental journey.

Below are some examples of early writing – how would you sequence the development of the writers from this, albeit limited, evidence?

Examples of pre-Level 1 writing

Example 1: all letters

I went to Blackpool on Sunday. Mum and Dad took me on the rides on the pleasure beach.

Example 2: very few letters

I went to my Nana's.

Example 3: range of letters

I like painting and drawing best.

All three examples are pre-communicative and cannot be deciphered by an adult. All three writers have stated what their writing says, but this is not necessary to our analysis. You probably identified example 2 as the least advanced. This writer has included some letters, but very few. The writer of example 3 is at a similar stage, but has included a greater range of letters, while example 1 is composed of all letters with no letter-like symbols.

How do we move children through these early stages?

The stages of early writing described above are characteristic of what we might see during the Foundation Stage and for some children, well into Year 1. Children need plenty of opportunities to practise independent writing and we need to be pro-active in developing writing from the mark-making stage. This could include:

- Free writing during role play – the emphasis may be on talk, but as part of the role play children could be encouraged to model the range of print they see around the home or the local community – a letter from the hospital, a map of the safari park, a menu, a Christmas card, a supermarket notice etc.

- Focus on trying to move children's attempts from the 'mark-making' to the 'random letters' stage by linking the phonic work that is taught throughout Reception and Year 1. For example, each time children need a word, ask them what it starts with or what sounds they can hear in the word so that you are reinforcing letter knowledge through the writing context.

- Present children with varied writing activities (e.g. prose, lists and simple charts) to get the message across that all writing does not look the same.

- Link writing activities to personal interests and needs as far as possible. For example, remember that even at this stage boys may be inspired by different topics than girls, and we need to represent the full range of cultures.

- Use varied writing tools and materials – coloured paper rather than boring white, thick markers rather than plain pencil and so on.

- Use ICT activities wherever possible.

As the writing becomes sprinkled with letter-like shapes and some legibly written letters, move it on by:

- Asking the child to read out his/her writing in order to emphasise the purpose of the message – What is it? Who is it for? Why does the child need to send this message to that person?

- Linking his/her efforts to models in the classroom and elsewhere around the learning environment.

- Talking about letters and words (the difference between these).

- Talking about letter names and linking these to the sounds and shapes.

As these early attempts show a greater awareness of letters and words as the basis of writing, continue with the strategies suggested above and at the same time seek to develop a more strategic placing of letters to represent words – for example, focus on the first sound in a word, then the last sound, then the middle vowel as children appear ready for this, alongside the word work that is taught during the literacy hour.

At the earliest stages, the links between writing and spelling are more pronounced. There is a sense in which writing is mainly spelling as the serious work on sentence structure has not yet got going at this emergent stage, and the main teaching emphasis is on securing the letter sounds and shapes.

P scales, early learning goals and National Curriculum Level 1

The small steps of development that characterise early writing may have come as a surprise if you have not already experienced children's writing in the Foundation Stage and in Key Stage 1. Having looked briefly at how early writing progresses, you may now find it helpful to match the above descriptions to the P scales (DfES 2001) that have only recently been devised to measure writing progress below and within Level 1 of the National Curriculum. These are intended mainly to measure the progress of children with special educational needs, but the P scales reflect the stages of early writing and help us to see clearly how early writing leads into Level 1 of the National Curriculum. The P scales also reflect the early learning goals for the Foundation Stage (see below).

Consider the descriptions of writing summarised in the boxes below. There are eight levels from P1 to P8 (P1 is the lowest). Consider also the writing objectives from the early learning goals that are intended to lead into Level 1 of the National Curriculum.

Summary of the P scale descriptors

P1–3   The earliest levels of 'scribble' and very basic mark-making (without meaning).

P4   Pupils understand that marks and symbols convey meaning, for example, 'scribble writing alongside a picture'.

P5   Pupils produce some meaningful print, signs or symbols... associated with their own name or familiar spoken words... They make and complete patterns (handwriting).

P6   Pupils differentiate between letters and symbols.

P7   Pupils group letters and leave spaces between them as though they are separate words. Some letters are correctly formed. They are aware of the sequence of letters, symbols and words.

P8   In their writing... pupils... use familiar words and letters in sequence to communicate meaning, showing awareness of different purposes – letters, lists, stories or instructions.

Writing objectives from the early learning goals

Writing is included within the section on 'Communication, Language and Literacy'. By the end of the Foundation Stage (Reception), children are expected to:

- Attempt writing for different purposes, using features of different forms such as lists, stories and instructions.
- Write their own names and other things such as labels and captions, and begin to form simple sentences, sometimes using punctuation.

Many of the P scale phrases and the statements from the early learning goals reflect how we have described the stages of early writing – as basic mark-making progresses towards 'letter-like shapes' and hence to legibly written letters within writing that starts to communicate a message. Using the P scale descriptors and/or the early learning goals, how would you assess the examples of early writing shown on pages 19–20? Don't worry if you struggled to find a 'best fit' for each piece – few pieces of writing fall neatly into such boxes. In my view, these three writers are working within Level P6 and with more correctly formed letters and spaces between the attempted words would be well on the way to achieving Level P7.

Once pupils have progressed through the P levels and the early learning goals they are working within Level 1 of the National Curriculum. Consider the objectives for this:

Summary of writing objectives at Level 1 of the National Curriculum

At Level 1C, pupils' writing:
- Communicates meaning – through simple words and phrases.
- Still needs to be mediated to be understood.
- Includes some letters that are clearly shaped but may not be consistent in their size and **orientation**.

At Level 1B, the writing has progressed towards:
- Being generally understood by adults without the child's 'help'.
- Having some full stops (even if these are not consistently used).
- Including recognisable, if simple, statements to communicate ideas.
- Most letters being clearly shaped and correctly oriented.

At Level 1A, pupils' writing should include:
- Some words that are spelt conventionally (e.g. the **tricky, high-frequency words** such as I, said, he, for).
- Some choices of appropriate vocabulary.
- Some use of capital letters and full stops.

Below are some examples of writing at a later stage. How would you match these to the Level 1 descriptors?

Examples of writing at Level 1

Example 1

ToM cte is o a mt K

Tom's cat is on a motorbike.

Example 2

LaST nayT I WenT to My NaNLiNS
        night   Nan's

I pLiD aLiTL Gim .... Nan FraNSi's
  played   game

ProMiST The AT I cuD Go to pichs I puT
               could   pictures

on My cuwT and asc awr GraNDAD
      coat   asked our

if he woNTiD to cum. He sed now.
      wanted   come   said   no

Again, don't worry if you found it hard to decide where each piece of writing fits. All we can do is to assign a 'best fit'. I would match example 1 to Level 1C as the writing still needs to be mediated to be understood by the reader. Example 2 I would place at 1B as the message can be deciphered without mediation and there is evidence of full stops. This writer has produced some simple statements to communicate his ideas but does not yet spell many of the high-frequency words correctly (for 1A).

So what do the writers at Level 1 need in order to move them on to the next level? To answer this question we could look at the National Curriculum objectives for Level 2 as this is what we would be aiming towards:

Writing at Level 2

At this level the child:
- Uses narrative and non-narrative forms of writing.
- Uses appropriate and interesting vocabulary.
- Shows some awareness of readers.
- Sequences sentences together showing knowledge of how full stops and capital letters are used.
- Spells most monosyllabic words correctly and represents other words using plausible alternatives.
- Forms letters correctly that are consistent in size.

As we can see, writing moves on considerably between National Curriculum Level 1 and Level 2. How we can help learners to progress from early writing, and through to Level 4 and beyond, forms the content of the following chapters.

Generally speaking, early writing refers mainly to that prior to Level 1 and the point of this exploration is for you to understand the very small steps of progression that characterise this.

Developmental versus traditional approaches to writing

If you are mature in years, you may have been taught to write using a traditional approach, unlike younger people who are more likely to have learned to write through the developmental approach. Does it matter how we learn to write? Which method is best for children? Consider what I think are the characteristics of traditional and developmental approaches to writing – how would you sort them into 'traditional' and 'developmental'?

Traditional and developmental approaches to supporting writing

1 Over-reliance on copying.
2 Involves thinking.
3 Leaves scope for experimentation and risk-taking.

4   Writing is over-corrected.

5   Learners are afraid to be 'wrong'.

6   Writing is mainly directed by adults.

7   Writer is given spellings to copy.

8   Writing is often shared – for example, pairs of pupils writing together.

9   Writing is often solitary.

10 Writer develops a 'have-a-go' attitude to writing and spelling.

11 Writing is for a real audience.

12 The learners sometimes choose their own topic and purpose.

13 Writers are confident and share their efforts with peers and adults.

14 Learners are more likely to develop anxiety if they can't 'do it'.

15 Learners acquire more independence from the beginning.

You may have assigned numbers 2, 3, 8, 10, 11, 12, 13 and 15 to developmental approaches and the rest to traditional approaches – or you may not. A debate on what is traditional as opposed to developmental would trigger many disagreements and you may well disagree with my choices. Similarly, which method or approach to writing is the 'best' for children is also open to debate.

As writing develops, we need a balance of both approaches to get children started and instil in them positive attitudes towards writing. We want young learners to be motivated, inspired, excited, confident, and to understand the creativity and potential of writing. Even if, for some learners, these feelings and attitudes wane during the later stages, we can at least make a positive start.

A strong argument for developmental writing is offered by Bayley and Day (2003). With reference to copy writing, and accepting that some copy writing is necessary, for example, for handwriting, 'if children habitually copy the adult's writing, they will not have the opportunity to reveal what they know'. Further, 'children who are encouraged to produce their own unaided writing are more likely to see themselves as writers and develop a positive attitude to writing'. I agree – over the years I have seen many children hide behind the copying habit and sadly watched them fail to become *thinking* writers.

I also favour the developmental approach for the following reasons:

- The learner whose writing is covered with corrections will soon lose heart, especially if motivation is in short supply from the start. On the other hand, the learner who is never corrected will not progress. What is needed is sensitive and purposeful guidance that reflects the objectives being focused on during a particular lesson, for example, if the focus is on punctuation then why identify all the spelling mistakes? These could be left for another time when spelling is the focus.

- Writers who are afraid to be wrong will struggle to develop an experimental approach to writing. They will be afraid to take risks. Yet risk-taking is an essential feature of learning anything. Children need to know that mistakes are not only allowed but *expected* as part of the learning experience. And as long as they use their errors to inform and develop learning, the risk-takers will, because of their less anxious approach to writing, progress faster than those learners who fear being wrong.

- Similarly, children who are given spellings to copy are unlikely to develop their own spelling strategies. Writing at all levels depends for its free flow on children not stopping continually for help with spellings. I would never give a spelling, unless it is part of helping the child to spell tricky words, as part of the **Look, Say, Cover, Write, Check (LSCWC)** strategy.

- Traditionalist approaches have often relied on copying and adult-initiated topics with very little choice or recognition of diversity (e.g. boys writing about 'girly' topics) and a lack of original thought. The major emphasis has traditionally been on grammar and structure rather than on content and interest with the use of colourful vocabulary. While there is still an emphasis on grammar and structure through the NLS objectives, developmental writing also recognises that grammar and structure are not the be all and end all of good writing. Inspiration comes from children knowing that their thoughts and ideas form the backbone of the writing.

Similarly, writing need not always be a solitary activity. Why not have paired writing sessions on occasions, especially if some children need support and confidence? The purpose of this section is to draw attention to the issues that can help or hinder children's to progress.

Teaching assistants supporting writing

Although this chapter is concerned with early writing, it is important to establish from the start how teaching assistants can support all levels. We need to start children off with healthy attitudes and perceptions of writing. In my view there are three main strands:

- To guide – sensitively and with regard to the pace of individual learning.
- To model – allow learners to see good examples of what is required.
- To facilitate – through a positive learning environment.

All adults need to know what is to be guided, modelled and facilitated. While the National Curriculum prescribes through broad descriptors what aspects of writing are to be measured, focused writing sessions are driven by the requirements of the NLS (2001), now the Primary Strategy (more on this in next three chapters).

The NLS objectives for teaching early writing

Consider the implications for supporting early writing through the NLS framework. This is based around a philosophy of:

- Inclusion – children learn better with their peers.
- High expectations for all children – therefore every child can become a writer given the right learning environment.
- Entitlement – all children are entitled to receive quality teaching and support.

The objectives for teaching are based around:

- Word level – spelling and vocabulary.
- Sentence level – how words fit together to form sentences.
- Text level – how sentences link to form paragraphs and longer pieces of writing.

The next three chapters are based around these objectives; without some knowledge of how these drive the teaching of writing in most schools, supporting writing will be less effective.

How children think about writing

Finally, learners have much to tell us about how to support their development of writing. Consider the comments from some children below. Which have been made by struggling or reluctant writers and which have been made by competent writers? What do they tell us about their feelings?

Children's comments about writing

I never finish my stories.
A proper writer came to talk...she writes all day (accompanied by a look of amazement).
Writing is...letters – they make words.
I can't think of anything to write about.
I can't remember how to write letters.
Writing is what my teacher does.
Writing makes my hand hurt.
Writing is...like lists and stories and things.

Adults have the power to shape children's thoughts from the start. The emphasis on small steps is all-important. From the beginning, all children need to experience success, and gaps in knowledge, however small, need to be filled in as soon as they are observed. Letter knowledge is a particular sticking point – those children who emerge from their early writing experiences with letter confusions face a huge barrier to further learning.

This chapter has presented early writing as an essential foundation for more in-depth and formal work in the later stages. For those of you who support mainly at this early level and wish to enhance your knowledge, further information and suggestions (including CD) are provided through the NLS document *Developing Early Writing* (DfES 2001).

Summary

In this chapter I have looked at:

● The characteristics of early writing.

● The small steps of progression that constitute early writing.

● Some strategies and suggestions for moving early writing forward.

● Tools for measuring progress in early writing.

● The role of the teaching assistant in developing writing.

● Children's perceptions of themselves as writers.

Chapter 4

Supporting writing at sentence level

An obvious characteristic of early writing is the lack of any clear distinction between words, sentences and text. The writing considered in the previous chapter featured mark-making that progresses gradually towards a random mass of letters, representing the writer's attempts to communicate meaning. In general, early writing does not yet demonstrate any one-to-one correspondence between the intended message and what appears on the page.

Some discussion on spelling has been appropriate in the context of early writing (see *Supporting Spelling* in this series, which contains a wealth of information and practical suggestions for those who wish to explore further). This chapter discusses the complexities of writing, progressing from word to sentence level, grammar and Standard English, different purposes for sentences, and punctuation. We will also consider examples of the NLS objectives that drive writing at sentence level together with some suggestions for activities.

Writing as a complex activity

What do you think about when you write? Consider the sub-skills for writing listed below as you reflect on your own writing.

The sub-skills of writing		
Word level	**Sentence level**	**Text level**
Spelling	Use of Standard English	Purpose
Vocabulary	Grammar/syntax	Audience
Letter formation	Punctuation	Format/style

Even at word level the writer has to think about spelling, choices of vocabulary and neat handwriting. Yet, most of what we ask children to do is at sentence and text levels, which involves thinking about grammar and punctuation, and at text level, the audience and the purpose of the written piece. The complexity of the activity is awesome: the ultimate in multi-tasking!

Consider then how it is for learners. Of course, not all writing brings into play every sub-skill listed in the box above – handwriting and the accuracy of the spelling do not matter in a shopping list. At word level there is no need to bother about grammar – these are issues of presentation for readers. Similarly, when we write in our diaries we are our own audience.

At sentence and text levels, different sub-skills take centre stage according to the type of text being written, its audience and what the text is intended to do. What is the difference between a letter to Grandma in hospital and a letter of complaint to a company informing them that you have found a beetle in their tin of tuna? Both pieces of writing will probably adhere to the general format of a letter, but the language and the tone (use of grammar) will be different. Consider the two letters below – how are they different?

> Dear Grandma
> How are you? I hope you're feeling much better after your operation. We can't wait to come over and see you at the weekend. Hope you like the flowers.
>
> Love and kisses
>
> Sylvia and the family

> Dear Sir
> I am writing to return a tin of tuna that I bought from the Better shop on Goodwill Street, Hightown, on the 19th August 2004. Please note the remains of a dead beetle inside the tin.

Having bought many tins of your brand of tuna over the years, I have always expected high quality and received it. I have never experienced this kind of thing before. In fact your tuna has always been of the highest standard.

I am writing to inform you so that you can ensure that this does not happen to your other customers.

Yours faithfully

Mrs A Fish

You may have noticed that the letter to Grandma (informal):

- uses a 'loose' sentence structure – the grammar is not always correct;
- uses short forms of words (e.g. *you're* and *can't*);
- has a warmer tone to the message;
- contains a different repertoire of vocabulary;
- uses shorter sentences.

The audience (Grandma) is not bothered about the presentation – all she wants to receive is a comforting letter that will help her to feel better. But with regard to that beetle in the tuna – what we want from our writing is a result, ideally in the form of some free products as compensation! A dozen tins of tuna would be a wonderful outcome. I'm sure you get the drift.

Of course, we do not consciously separate all the sub-skills when we write, but at sentence and text levels we need to make the right choices. The following sections focus on how we can help children to write good sentences.

How we construct sentences

What is a sentence? Many children have no idea what a sentence is, even when they are trying to compose one. Adults constantly say things such as

'Let's put that word into a sentence' or 'Write two or three sentences about what you did over the weekend.'

Do you agree that a sentence:

- is composed of one or more words?
- should make sense as a unit of meaning?
- reflects spoken language?
- is demarcated by full stops?
- has a specific purpose and part to play within a piece of text?

Some NLS objectives for simple sentence writing are listed below:

NLS objectives for simple sentence writing

Children should be taught:
- That a line of writing is not necessarily the same as a sentence (Y1, T1) – many children misunderstand this.
- To write captions and simple sentences and to reread, recognising whether or not they make sense, for example, missing words, word order (Y1, T1).
- To reinforce knowledge of the term 'sentence' from previous terms (Y1, T3).
- About word order, by reordering sentences, predicting words from previous text, grouping a range of words that might 'fit' and discussing the reasons why.
- To secure the use of simple sentences in own writing (Y2, T2).

The *Oxford Concise Dictionary* defines a sentence as a 'set of words complete in itself, as an expression of thought'. The key is grammar. Our knowledge of grammar comes to life when we write a sentence. So, if you are one of those people who have never been taught grammar, sit back for a quick whizz through the basics as we consider what children need to know in order to write effective sentences.

Word classes

Within a sentence words perform different functions, for example:

- **Nouns** name things – *cat, dog, table, phone, television, window, car.*
- **Adjectives** describe nouns – *big, green, bright, sleek, pretty.*
- **Verbs** are the 'doing' words – *think, write, spell, jumping, barked, eaten.*
- **Adverbs** describe the verbs – *quickly, beautifully, loudly, softly.*
- **Prepositions** describe where things are – *in, on, by, under, around, with.*
- **Pronouns** often act instead of nouns – *he, she, they, it, which.*
- **Conjunctions** join short sentences together – *and, then, if, because, but.*
- **Determiners** are the little words that don't mean much by themselves – *the, a, me, that* – but when placed with other words determine the meaning of the sentence.

Some examples from the NLS objectives that focus particularly on word classes are listed below.

NLS objectives for word classes

Children should be taught:
- The function of verbs in sentences, noticing that sentences cannot make sense without them (Y3, T1).
- To use verb tenses with increasing accuracy in speaking and writing (Y3, T1).
- The function of adjectives within sentences (Y3, T2).
- To identify pronouns and understand their function in sentences (Y3, T3).
- To investigate verb tenses (past, present and future) (Y4, T1).
- To identify adverbs and investigate their functions in sentences (Y4, T1).
- To understand the significance of word order (Y4, T2).
- The use of connectives (*if, then, so*) to structure an argument (Y4, T3).
- To search for, identify and classify a range of prepositions...experiment with substituting different prepositions and their effects on meaning. Understand and use the term 'preposition' (Y5, T3).

Most of this intense work on the functions of different kinds of words happens in most schools throughout Years 3 and 4.

Help children to understand word classes by:

- Dictating simple sentences that focus on particular word classes, for example, *The dog ran.* Ask children if it is a complete sentence that makes sense.

- Gradually extending the word classes and using the terms 'noun' or 'verb' accordingly. You might focus on sentences with adjectives – *The big, hungry dog ran* – or on adverbs – *The dog ran quickly.*

- Adding other word classes, for example, prepositions – *The big, hungry dog ran quickly through the street.*

- Using colourful word cards to identify word classes – a set of noun cards in pink, verb cards in yellow and so on, for children to make up sentences. The use of colour helps children to separate each word class.

- Sorting different categories within the same word class – for example, adjectives into those of colour, size or shape.

- Underlining or highlighting particular word classes in a photocopied, short piece of text – for example, highlight the nouns in one colour, verbs in another, adverbs in another and so on.

- Substituting different words within the same word class – ask children to change the verb/noun/adjective in a sentence. How is their sentence changed?

- Collecting examples of word classes from books and texts that are currently part of their curricular reading and writing – nouns from history, verbs from science, adjectives from art and so on, and identifying these in 'cross-curricular' sentences that already mean something to the children.

- Collecting an assortment of words and categorising them into word classes – children could then write them onto coloured word cards themselves for the activities suggested above.

Try not to promote bad habits by encouraging children to link long strings of adjectives and adverbs – professional writers prefer to let the nouns and verbs speak for themselves.

Always focus on sentences making sense. Check by asking 'Do these words go together as a set of words within themselves, to express a thought?' They could test their sentence by drawing a picture to go with it – if the sentence expresses a thought, there should be some image that can be drawn.

Try not to use pencil and paper all of the time. Card activities enable some children who find writing difficult to focus on meaning and 'what a sentence is' without handwriting problems inhibiting their thinking.

Using pronouns

Pronouns allow us to vary how we refer to people and things. This is something children may find difficult. Pronouns (*she, it, they*) can tend to remove immediate reference from the person or thing (Mum, the rabbit, Auntie Carole and Uncle John), and may place a veil over the meaning of a sentence if overused. Pronouns eliminate the need to keep repeating the same noun.

We can help children to understand and use pronouns in writing by:

● Ensuring that they understand them and use them in speech.

● Focusing on pronouns through card activities – make two sets of word cards, one of pronouns and one of a range of nouns, for children to match up, for example, *Mum* to *she*, or *it* to *the dog*.

● Pointing out where pronouns can be substituted when responding to children's written work.

● Talking about pronouns in sentences and looking at models.

Using prepositions

There are about 100 prepositions in English, the most common being:

of	in	to	with	as	at	for	on	by	from

Prepositions often have meanings that are subtle and complex. They also have different purposes within sentences:

● Place – *at, on, in, inside, within, outside, by, near, behind, above, below, across, along, past, round.*

- Time – *at, in, on, during, for, after, before, since.*
- Reason – *because of, despite, for, with.*
- Similarity – *as, like, unlike.*

As you can see, the same preposition can denote time or place:

> I'll meet you *at* ten o'clock.
> I'll meet you *at* the main clock in the square.

Help children to understand prepositions through some of the activities and strategies already mentioned.

Meaning-carrying words and determiners

Children need to understand the difference between words that carry meaning in their sentences and the 'determiners' that join them together. Without the meaning-carrying words thought cannot be expressed, but without the determiners, the sentence is not complete grammatically. I often call determiners the *function* words as their function is to support the meaning-carrying words.

You may notice that many of the determiners listed in the box below are prepositions.

Function words (from NLS list)

as	at	by	in	on	the	and	like	I	said

The list of words may be familiar as the NLS tricky words. Think about these words and ask yourself:

- What is the meaning of each word?
- Can I join many of these words together to form a sentence?
- Does each word express a thought?
- Can a child draw a picture to go alongside any sentences using these groups of words only?

You probably placed some words together but they are unlikely to express much thought. Help children to understand the difference between 'function' and 'meaning-carrying' words by:

- Giving them simple sentences or phrases with meaning-carrying words only for them to fill in the determiners. This will reinforce their understanding of how the two sets of words combine in sentences and the function of each set of words.

- Giving them sentences with the determiners only for them to add the meaning-carrying words – this activity will be more difficult.

- Using coloured word cards again – one colour for the function words and another for the meaning-carrying words – children should make up sentences with the focus on meaning. The colour helps them to notice what each set of words is doing in each sentence.

- Reinforcing knowledge of word classes as you go along – how many nouns does your sentence have? How many adjectives?

Focusing on the differences between meaning-carrying words and determiners helps children to see how the sets of words complement each other in sentences.

Same word – different meaning

Within a sentence the same word can have different meanings. Consider:

- We had our coffee in the *green* room. / The *green* was too wet for golf.
- *Turn* around. / It's your *turn* next. / The man did a *turn* at the concert.
- *Go* down to the chemist. / I want to have a *go*.

These are just some examples of the many words in English from which meaning is gleaned only from the sentence itself. In the examples above, the words in italics can be nouns, adjectives or verbs, depending on their meaning in the sentence.

Help children to understand how words change their meaning. They could:

- Write different sentences that include the same word.

- Be shown models of sentences that show the same words as verbs, nouns or adjectives.
- Collect, as investigation-type activities, examples of words that can be used to change the meaning of sentences.

Children will only catch on to these if they have opportunities to talk about the meaning of these sets of words. Make a fuss when you come across one by making them silly – laughter aids memory.

Verb tenses

A significant element of sentence-making is the ability to use verb structures correctly. Let's look at the main ones without going too much into the complexities. Consider the following:

- The man is *running*. / I *run* every day.
- Last year we *went* to Spain for our holidays. We *were going to visit* Portugal, but we *changed* our minds. I *have already visited* many of the countries in Europe.
- Next year we *are going* to Florida. We *will be* in Florida for two weeks.
- If I *had known it was going* to rain I *would have* brought my umbrella.
- That job *should have been done* by now.

The first example is a simple one. Sometimes we use the present continuous form of the verb to denote an activity that is ongoing – for example, *is running, is jumping, is eating*. At other times we may use the simple form of the verb – *run, jump, eat, go, read* or *write*.

The past tense of verbs, as in the second example, is relatively simple for most children, but note the number of versions. Many children in Key Stage 1 have not yet grasped the irregular versions of verbs and will apply a past tense rule in error – for example, 'goed' for went, and 'sawed' for seen.

In the third example, the future tense is often more problematic for children. Verb structures that include *would, could* and *should* often cause immense problems for some children for whom spoken language does not include these more complex tenses.

Consider the text in the box below. You might wish to classify the verbs as present, past and so on. This type of activity is good for children who have a range of verbs as part of their spoken language repertoire and who have reached this level of thinking about verbs in sentences.

Combining different verb structures

We visited Florida last August. We had a wonderful time, but hadn't known it was the rainy season. It rained every day. One day, we were at the theme park and it bucketed down. You've never seen such a downpour. Paige laughed and jumped in the puddles, and we all sang 'Singing in the Rain', much to the amusement of some of the other visitors. After that, we each decided to buy one of those yellow ponchos with Mickey Mouse pictured on the back. The holiday was wonderful, but if we do go again, we will try to avoid the rainy season.

Children can be helped to use different verb structures in their writing by:

- Seeing different models around the classroom from different areas of the curriculum.
- Highlighting particular verbs in texts.
- Categorising verb structures into the different tenses.
- Using verb cards to make their own sentences.
- Talking about verb structures in the context of other learning.

From words to phrases to sentences

Let's look at how words combine. Just as single words can be classed as nouns, verbs and so on, phrases do a similar job using more than one word. Consider the following:

- A **verb chain** (phrase) does the job of a verb – *is dancing, was eating, has been writing.*
- A **noun phrase** does the job of a noun – *the large dog, my ham sandwich.*
- An **adverbial phrase** works like an adverb to describe the verb. How did he run? *As fast as a hare, without looking back.*

- An **adjectival phrase** works like an adjective to describe the noun – the TV *with the flickering switch, the dress as red as fire.*

Help children to link words into phrases by:

- Providing lots of models and using these in sentences.
- Collecting examples and categorising them into noun, verb, adverb, adjectival or prepositional phrases.
- Playing 'Happy Families' with word cards that combine into phrases.
- Placing halves of phrases together that have been 'jigsawed'.

Try to reinforce other learning as far as possible. For example, word cards are likely to include the function words that are included within the NLS list of tricky words that children have to learn.

Children who find it difficult to write complete sentences may find it less daunting to make phrases at first. What matters is that children recognise the need for words to combine as chunks of meaning. The box below contains a mixture of single words, phrases and sentences – think about what they each convey as chunks of meaning.

Chunks of meaning

Words	Phrases	Sentences
Black	The black dog	The black dog stole the sausage.
Cat	My pet cat	Sadly, my pet cat died last week.
Strong	A strong hutch	Dad made a strong hutch for my rabbit.
Gobble	He gobbled	He gobbled that huge peanut butter sandwich in ten seconds.
Without	Without hesitation	Without hesitation, John jumped into the water.

You might ask yourself:

- Which word classes are included?

- Which are the noun phrases, verb phrases and so on?
- Within the sentences, how are the function words and meaning-carrying words combined?
- Thinking about the meanings, can you create an image in your mind from each phrase, sentence or word?

From simple to complex sentences

Words and phrases combine into **clauses**. A simple sentence is made up of one clause, as in:

- The dog bit the man.
- He ran away.
- The bite got infected.
- He had to go to hospital.

Each of the above sentences conveys a single thought or idea.

A **complex sentence** consists of more than one clause, as in:

- When the man got bitten *he had to go to hospital.*
- As the wound became infected *it made the man ill.*
- *The dog owner decided to put his dog down* because it had bitten a man.

In each example there is more than one thought or idea expressed within the sentence. The main idea should stand on its own as a chunk of meaning as do the examples in italics – those clauses not in italics cannot stand alone as complete sentences.

Consider the examples from the NLS objectives for writing complex sentences listed below before we explore the implications.

Examples of NLS objectives for complex sentence writing

Children should be taught:
- To find examples...of words and phrases that link sentences (Y2, T1).

- To reread their own writing to check for grammatical sense (coherence) and accuracy (agreement) – identify errors and suggest alternative constructions (Y2, T2).
- How sentences can be joined in more complex ways through using a widening range of conjunctions (Y3, T3).
- To investigate effects of substituting adverbs in clauses or sentences (Y4, T1).
- To adapt writing for different readers and purposes by changing vocabulary, tone and sentence structures, for example, simplifying for younger readers (Y5, T1).
- To construct sentences in different ways while retaining meaning (Y5, T3).
- To investigate clauses (Y5, T3).
- To use connectives to link clauses within sentences and to link sentences in longer texts (Y5, T3).
- The construction of complex sentences (Y6, T1).
- To form complex sentences using different connecting devices (Y6, T1).

Let's explore briefly some of the above areas.

Conjunctions

Think about how simple sentences can become compound or complex sentences by the use of **conjunctions**. I have often referred to these as 'joining words' when working with children. You can probably add more conjunctions to the following list:

and   but   or   when   although   if   because   unless   while

Consider the following sentences that use conjunctions to join two units of thought:

- The children went on a school trip *and* had a good time.
- I want to go out *but* Mum and Dad won't let me.

- I'm going to do my homework *then* I'll go out to play.
- They went on the train *because* the car had broken down.
- *Although* it was raining, she still went for a walk.
- *If* the shop is still open, I'll go for some bread.

The first three examples are probably the most common. We are used to seeing sentences written by children that overuse the word *and*, for example, *We went to the Railway Museum and it was good and then we had our lunch and then we came home and it rained* and so on. Many children get carried away when they are writing a story or recounting a string of events and end up with sentences peppered with 'and' or 'then', or other joining words that have been misapplied.

Help children to understand conjunctions and to use them appropriately by:

- Finding examples for children to study and use as models.
- Talking about the meanings of conjunctions, for example, the word *but* implies an opposite line of thought; the word *because* implies a cause and effect relationship.
- Playing games that focus on conjunctions – for example, make word cards for a range of conjunctions. Children have to invent sentences to fit each one.
- Joining simple sentences together using conjunctions.
- Using conjunctions wrongly – children spot the deliberate mistake.

Relative clauses

A further feature of complex sentences is the use of words such as *which*, *who*, *whom* and *that*. These words initiate **relative clauses** that give more information about a noun, for example:

- The kind man, *who* helped to chase the thief, received a medal.
- Aunt Millie, *who* we know has won the lottery, says she can't afford to go on holiday.

These words start off clauses that are often slipped into the middle of a sentence and need a comma at each end.

Subject, verb and object

A further point about clauses: every clause has a **subject** and a **verb** (SV). Many sentences have a subject, verb and an **object** (SVO).

The man was throwing.	The man threw the ball.
Children are eating.	Children eat too many crisps and chips.
Bob was washing.	Bob was washing his car.

The sentences on the left are SV sentences as they have a subject and a verb, but no object: there is no one/nothing to whom/which any action is done. The ones on the right are SVO sentences as they each have an object: the man threw to *someone*; the children eat *something*; Bob washed *something*.

The man (subject), threw (verb), the ball (object).
Children (subject), eat (verb), too many crisps and chips (object).
Bob (subject), was washing (verb), his car (object).

Reflexive verbs

Consider the following verb structures in relation to the subject, verb and object:

We all sleep.
The children think.
We have a shower.
We get dressed every morning.

Have you noticed that these verbs describe what we do to ourselves? We don't sleep to somebody else. We can only think to ourselves. We dress ourselves. These types of verbs are **reflexive** as the subject and object are the same (ourselves).

Thankfully we don't analyse our sentences in terms of subjects, verbs and objects – most of the time we simply write from our knowledge of spoken language. But we need to know the basics of grammar if we are to analyse children's sentences and put them onto the right track.

Active or passive

According to the required formality of a piece of writing, the verbs we use may be **active** or **passive**. Consider the following sets of sentences.

The dog bit the man. / The man was bitten by the dog.
Betty is eating an ice cream. / The ice cream is being eaten by Betty.
The teacher gave out the books. / Books were given out by the teacher.

The sentences on the left are active sentences and simply state who did what, while the ones on the right are passive as they state what is or was done to something or someone in a less direct way. The person (or thing) who 'did it' is not always stated. In passive sentences, that something or someone can be unknown or generalised. We can write:

The man has been bitten.
The papers were brought to the meeting.
The evidence was examined.
The house was burgled and some valuable paintings were stolen.

It is not stated *who* did it, simply that an action was done. The passive voice is often used to write more formal pieces such as science or newspaper reports. The point of using the passive voice is to record what happened, not who did it, as the 'who' is often not known anyway. Perhaps as you read on you will find yourself noticing when I use the passive voice in this book (quite a lot).

Children can be helped (passive?) to understand different sentence structures and verb tenses by:

- Seeing different examples around them and being helped to understand the purpose of each type of structure.

- Changing verbs from the active to the passive tense (within the context of when the passive tense is used).

- Colour – make sets of cards with the passive verbs clearly identified by colour for children to put together.

- Searching for deliberate mistakes – for example, the children could correct the wrong verbs.

- Talking about active and passive voices and sentence structures perhaps in small group or paired sentence-making sessions. Children then collaborate on their composition of sentences according to given criteria, for example, they have to compose a simple or a complex sentence in the active or passive voice and so on.

Children should not be encouraged to write compound or complex sentences if they cannot yet write simple ones as confusions are likely to become compounded.

Bringing sentences to life

We have seen how the rules of grammar affect the way in which sentences are written. We can, if we have the skills and knowledge, vary our sentences and bring them to life by:

- Changing the nouns and verbs to make them more interesting.
- Adding adjectives and adverbs (sparingly) to modify the nouns and verbs.
- Varying the sequence of words in some types of sentences.
- Using a range of conjunctions to create longer sentences.

Consider the differences between the following pairs:

The boy ate his tea. / John enjoyed his fish and chips.
The boy ate his tea. / The fat boy in the baseball cap wolfed down six sausages.
The boy ate his tea. / Although he hated sprouts, the boy ate his tea.

While we may justifiably criticise the intense focus on grammar promoted by the NLS, some grammar needs to be explicitly taught in a sensitive and enjoyable way.

Dialogue in sentences

Consider the examples from the NLS objectives that refer to dialogue:

Examples from NLS objectives for use of dialogue

Children should be taught:

- To understand the difference between direct and reported speech (Y5, T1).
- To be aware of the differences between spoken and written language (Y5, T2).
- To understand how dialogue is set out, for example, on separate lines for alternative speakers (Y5, T2).

Direct speech is when we write the exact words that people say and place them within speech marks, whereas **reported speech** expresses what is said in a less direct way. Consider the following examples.

Direct speech:	"Go away," she said.
Reported speech:	She told him to leave.

Dialogue need not follow the rules of grammar (I can almost hear your sigh of relief as you read this). Consider the following examples of dialogue:

- I'm going.
- Rain again!
- Yes, if you like.
- What would you like for tea?

Which examples make sense as complete units of meaning? The second example could be an exclamation that we make on a wet Sunday afternoon as we look out of the window and realise we can't cut the lawn. Grammatically we might say that those two words cannot make a sentence. On the other hand, they express a thought and convey the meaning quite well.

The dialogue parts of sentences can be, and often are, ungrammatical. They need to be if they are intended to reflect *real* speech patterns. Consider the following examples:

- "Get lost," she shouted.
- "Can I help you?" the lady in the library enquired.

We can sense the difference in emotion just by reading the dialogue. Sometimes we don't need to write 'he said' or 'she questioned' as the dialogue itself conveys who is speaking. Children need to be encouraged to write realistic dialogue and they can do this by:

● Experiencing different dialogue from characters in stories.
● Creating their own plays.
● Matching different types of dialogue to who has spoken.

Sentences have different purposes

The *Oxford Concise Dictionary* further defines the sentence as 'conveying a statement, question, exclamation or command'. Consider the examples from the NLS objectives that refer to sentence purpose.

NLS objectives that refer to sentence purpose

Children should be taught:
● To turn statements into questions (Y2, T3).
● To compare a variety of forms of questions (Y2, T3).
● To understand how the grammar of a sentence alters when the sentence type is altered, for example, when a statement is made into a question (Y4, T3).
● To understand how writing can be adapted for different audiences and purposes (Y5, T2).

Sentences can have different purposes and children need to understand this in order to write them. Study the examples below. Which are statements and which are questions? Which are exclamations and which are instructions? The punctuation marks are omitted deliberately.

Different kinds of sentences

1 Where are you going
2 I can't find the cat

---

3   A rough surface increases friction and slows down movement of an
    object
4   Wonderful
5   That's disgusting
6   Stand up and get in line
7   The sun shone onto the window
8   What time is it
9   Computer knowledge is an essential element of job specifications

---

How did you categorise them? Did you place numbers 4 and 5 in the exclamation category? Certainly, exclamations tend to be short bursts of meaning with few words. You probably identified number 6 as an instruction, numbers 1 and 8 as questions and the rest as statements.

Supporting children's sentence development is a complex task. The role of punctuation is a key factor in their understanding.

Punctuation

What does punctuation do for sentences? At a simple level, punctuation refers to capital letters, full stops, question marks and commas; at a more complex level, colons and semicolons. Punctuation marks act as cues, enabling the reader to make sense of a piece of text. Imagine what print would be like if sentences had no punctuation.

Consider the examples from the NLS framework for punctuation listed below: these provide an outline of how punctuation develops in writing.

NLS objectives for punctuation

Year 1, Term 1	To begin using full stops to demarcate sentences.
	To use a capital letter for 'I' and for the start of a sentence.
Year 1, Term 3	To add question marks to questions.
Year 2, Term 1	To use a variety of simple organisational devices, for example, arrows, lines, boxes, to indicate sequences and relationships.
	To reread own writing for sense and punctuation.

Year 2, Term 2	To identify speech marks...understand the purpose.
	To use commas to separate items in a list.
Year 3, Term 1	To secure knowledge of question marks and exclamation marks.
	To use speech punctuation correctly.
Year 3, Term 3	To note where commas occur in reading and to discuss their functions in helping the reader.
Year 4, Term 1	Use commas to mark grammatical boundaries within sentences.
Year 4, Term 2	Begin to use the apostrophe appropriately in own writing.
Year 4, Term 3	Recognise how commas...full stops join and separate clauses.
Year 5, Term 2	Use punctuation effectively to signpost meaning in complex sentences.
Year 6, Term 2	Secure understanding of more sophisticated punctuation marks – colon, semicolon, parenthetic commas, dashes, brackets.

The objectives for punctuation listed above show some developmental signposts for us to think about. Knowing where to put punctuation marks belongs with sentence work. If children don't know what a sentence is, they don't know where to put the full stop.

Let's consider commas for a moment as these sometimes cause difficulty. Are you a 'comma' person or not? I use commas a lot to add precise meaning to my sentences. Maybe I overuse them, but I am consciously trying to guide the reader by my use of commas. But, there is a saying 'when in doubt leave them out!' Consider the following uses for commas:

- In lists – I ate mash, beans, peas and carrots for tea.
- After speech – "I want some more," cried Oliver.
- In complex sentences – When I eat beans, I turn into Superman.
- For effect – I like mash, now and again.

Speech punctuation often causes problems, but these are generally more to do with the presence of dialogue as part of the sentence rather than the speech marks themselves. I have generally found that children remember where to put the 'sixty-sixes and ninety-nines' as long as they can identify the start and end of the speech.

Supporting punctuation

Help children to understand and use punctuation by:

- Linking punctuation marks clearly to sentence work.
- Ensuring that punctuation is taught at a pace at which individual children can cope.
- Leaving out punctuation from sentences and texts for children to fill in, at appropriate levels.
- Talking about why or why not to include a particular punctuation mark. This can work at all levels – from when to put in a full stop to when to use a comma for effect. Group debate on punctuation can work wonders for children's understanding.

General activities for promoting sentence skills

Below are a few more ideas:

- Teach children various ways to start a sentence, for example:
  - The subject – *The dog* frolicked in the sea.
  - A conjunction – *As* he frolicked, he barked and wagged his tail.
  - An adverb – *Excitedly*, the dog ran into the sea.
  - An adjective – *Excited* at seeing the sea, the dog ran in.
  - A phrase – *At the edge of the sea*, the dog wagged his tail and bounded in.
  - An 'ing' or 'ed' word – *Reaching* the edge of the sea, the dog ran into the water.
- Bring sentence work alive through drama and dressing up in general. Remember those children who need to learn through action.

- Use lots of visual aids – pictures, objects, art.
- Publish children's writing for others to read – one child was pleased to have his home-made book entitled *My Hamsters* placed in the book box for the rest of the class to read.
- Make sentence work short and sharp sometimes to encourage quick sentence writing. Children need to know that it's no good sitting there thinking of what to write for ten minutes and then finding that the time has disappeared. Sentence writing needs to be pencil-sharp.
- When making sentences, follow the cumulative principle – provide one word from which children have to create a sentence (e.g. *house* could become 'I live in a *house*'). Then progress to pairs of words (e.g. a noun and a verb) – *fish* and *bones* could become '*Fish* have back*bones*.' Choosing words that don't obviously go together may encourage adventurous sentence writing. Can you make a sentence with *flowers* and *diamonds*?
- Dictation is a good way to control the level of sentence structure you want a child to practise. This can then be followed by the child's own writing that models the structures that have been practised in a controlled situation.

Pie Corbett (in the *TES* in May 2002) suggests that we take the fuse out of the photocopier. I agree. Piles of worksheets may provide evidence that children have worked on the NLS objectives, but the writing often fails to match up. The proof is in the writing not the worksheet!

The sensitivities of Standard English

Sentence writing relies on knowledge of grammar, and grammar equates with using Standard English (SE). Consider the references to SE from the NLS objectives below.

NLS references to SE

Children should be taught:
- To use the basic conventions of Standard English and consider when and why Standard English is used (Y5, T1).
- To understand features of formal official language (Y6, T2).

But what do we really mean by SE? The first distinction is that between English used in the UK and English in other English-speaking countries. In many instances, the differences are those of vocabulary, for example, the use of the word 'sidewalk' for pavement in America.

In the UK we have different variations of English, some in the form of dialect and some in the form of accent. Accent is to do with how words are pronounced, for example, the word 'bath' in areas such as Lancashire (flat, short vowel sound) will be pronounced differently by people from many areas of the south. Dialect is the substitution of a different form of grammar, usually of the verb. Consider 'I were waiting while six for the train.' This is typical of some northern regions, for example, parts of Yorkshire. The SE version is 'I was waiting (or I waited) until six for the train.' Other examples include 'I been' or 'we was' and so on. The Year 5 NLS objective further refers to 'avoidance of non-standard dialect'. To some extent SE is standardised through formal text types, for example, science reports and legal documents.

The point of this section is to emphasise the sensitivity that needs to accompany work on SE. There are many variations of 'English' that deserve to be called SE, and SE used 50 years ago was nothing like what we consider as SE today.

All forms of community English deserve to be respected, and the development of writing in SE must work alongside what children bring to the writing context. Different forms of English contribute to a rich and varied writing curriculum.

In general, sentence work is enhanced by:

- Consideration of the principles outlined in Chapter 2.
- Modelling good examples that focus on specific objectives.
- Interactive tasks and activities that children enjoy.
- Talking about 'good sentences' and reflecting the issues so far explored in this chapter.
- Using examples from across the curriculum – sentence work should not be confined to literacy lessons.
- Using peer support when appropriate – two or more heads are sometimes better than one.

Much of this chapter has focused on grammar. Although suggestions for some activities have been offered, the message is clearly that we should avoid boring and meaningless exercises on grammar. The worst thing we can do for developing writers is to lift sentence work out of its language context by presenting them with tasks that are based on the parts without reference to the whole, wonderful, creative craft that is writing.

Summary

In this chapter I have looked at:

● Most of the essential attributes of sentence writing. If children cannot write sentences, they cannot write texts. In the past, we may have underestimated the importance of the sentence in our desire to encourage children to be creative. Yet creativity cannot flourish without the basic writing skills.

Chapter 5

Writing at text level: fiction

Let's move on to how sentences work together to build texts for fiction. This chapter aims to help you support the writing of:

● Stories

● Plays

● Poetry

Each section includes some of the NLS objectives that drive the teaching and learning of fiction writing.

Writing stories

What is a story? Most magazines (for women) contain short stories of various kinds that are intended as a single read, whereas novels are longer stories that we read over a period of weeks. Which **genres** do you like best?

● Crime

● Adventure

● Political thrillers

● Romance

● Historical

● Contemporary

● Regional sagas

Perhaps I have missed out your favourite. I personally enjoy reading political thrillers and historical novels (I am currently reading *Rebecca* by Daphne du Maurier).

So, why do children need to learn how to write stories? After all, very few children will eventually earn a living as authors. This is a tricky question. If we are helping children to write fiction then we are preparing them to write adult novels or short stories (as well as plays and poetry).

One part of the answer is because it is traditional and another is that fiction writing has the power to develop imaginative thinking. We could argue that by focusing on the writing we become more discerning and thoughtful readers. Telling stories is something we do all day. We recall and share personal experiences, interact socially and build and sustain friendships. In other words, stories are created from our own experiences and from what we observe.

Reluctant writers may ask the question: 'Why do I have to write a story?' And the answer cannot simply be 'because the NLS objectives tell us to' or 'because all children are assessed on it'. Children have a right to use their learning time to the best advantage, so fiction writing should at least offer opportunities for them to develop what they need and are interested in. Having said that, until children have been introduced to the full range of writing genres, they cannot know which is likely to interest them the most. Authors have a choice as to the subject matter and, to some degree, so should children. Let's now examine what good story writing involves.

Beginnings, middles and ends

All stories must have a beginning, middle and end. Consider the stories in the box below. They may be skeletons without flesh and bones, but they do have beginnings, middles and ends. They are typical of the shallow outlines that children often produce before they have learned how to give their storylines some depth and dimension.

Skeleton stories

1 Emma set off for school. She saw a fairy. The fairy waved her magic wand and took Emma off to a strange land. Then she brought her home again.
2 Jenny's bag was snatched. A passer-by chased the thief and got it back again.

> 3 John wouldn't eat his sprouts until one day, he discovered that they had special powers. Sprouts made him see into other people's minds. He used this secret to see into Paul's brain. But when he wrote down Paul's answers on the spelling test, he found that they were all wrong.
>
> 4 Carole set off for work. She bumped her car and had to go to the garage to get it mended. It cost her fifty pounds. Then she was on the road again.

These examples could be developed in different ways. For instance, what if, in story number 4, the garage man was a six-foot hunk and Carole's encounter sparked off a romance?

When writing stories children need to think about:

- What happens (plot).
- To whom it happens (characters).
- Where it happens (setting).
- When it happens (period in which the story is set).

The 'how' and 'why' of story writing are provided by the fleshing out of the characters and the depth and dimension given to the **plot** (and **sub-plots**).

Children also need to know about the main ingredient in story writing – **conflict**. If the key characters have no problem to solve, there is no story to be told. Books are sometimes written as a sequence of anecdotes, often touching or humorous, but these are not stories. Stories must have conflict and tension if they are to succeed (more on this later).

Before we go any further, let's consider the key areas for which children will need support.

Example NLS objectives for story writing from Key Stage 1

Year 1, Term 1	Write about events from personal experience.
	Make simple picture/story books to model book conventions.
	Write about significant incidents from known stories.
Year 1, Term 3	Write stories using simple settings.

| Year 2, Term 1 | Use language of time to structure a series of events. |
| Year 2, Term 3 | Write sustained stories: story elements, narrative, settings, characterisation and dialogue. |

Example NLS objectives for story writing from Key Stage 2

Year 3, Term 1	To develop use of settings in stories.
Year 3, Term 1	Write own passages of dialogue.
Year 3, Term 2	Describe and sequence key events.
	Write portraits of characters.
	Write alternative sequels to traditional stories, using same characters, settings, identifying typical phrases to structure writing.
Year 3, Term 3	Write openings to stories or chapters.
	Write a first person account.
Year 4, Term 1	Write character sketches ... focus on small details, to evoke sympathy or dislike.
	Write independently, linking own experience to historical stories. (How would I have responded?)
	Write more extended stories ... plan incidents and simple chapters.
	Use paragraphs to organise narrative.
Year 4, Term 2	Develop use of settings in own writing – using adjectives and figurative language.
Year 4, Term 3	Explore main issues of story – dilemma and issues it raises for characters.
	Write alternative endings for a known story – discuss how it would change the reader's view.
Year 5, Term 2	Write own versions of legends, myths and fables.
Year 5, Term 3	Write from another character's point of view.
	Write from the style of the author.
	Evaluate their work.
Year 6	Summarise a passage, chapter or longer text.
	Year 6 focuses on the fine details of writing stories and the speed of planning and writing.

Let's explore some of the key points from the objectives listed above.

Theme and plot

Most stories have a **theme** that epitomises what it is mainly about. For example, in the skeleton story examples above, we could say that the theme for story number 3 is that 'cheating always finds us out'.

Around the theme revolves the **plot** that relates the story through a sequence of events. When we ask a child 'what is your story about?' we are asking about its theme and its plot. The plot involves some kind of problem, and that important word, conflict. Most plots:

- Outline the character's problem.
- Describe how the character will solve the problem – the twists and turns that will prevent the character from solving the problem, i.e. the barriers in his/her way.
- Describe how the problem has been resolved.

Remember the story outline about Carole who bumped her car? Let's suppose she develops a relationship with the handsome hunk from the garage. All is well, until she finds out that he's married. She could persuade him to leave his wife. He agrees, and tells his wife of the relationship. But then, just as he's about to move in with Carole, his wife rushes out, gets in the car – she's upset, drives too fast, is involved in a nasty car accident. She ends up in hospital having lost her leg. The handsome hunk can't leave her now...or can he? What does his conscience tell him to do and how will Carole as the main character react to all these barriers standing in the way of her love life?

Many plots arise from the theme of searching for something and finding (or not finding) it. Problems arise from any area of life. Writers take what they can from their reading and invent more, so children need to be helped to think about their own experiences of life.

One of the most common shapes for plots is shown in the diagram below. We have an opening, or a 'hook' for the story, followed by a series of events and happenings that create suspense, followed by a climax when the character appears to have an insoluble problem as everything is conspiring against him/her. But, of course, as writers, we always have a trick up our sleeve to solve the character's problem – the resolution. Finally we have a satisfying ending to make the reader say 'Aah, yes' with a huge grin.

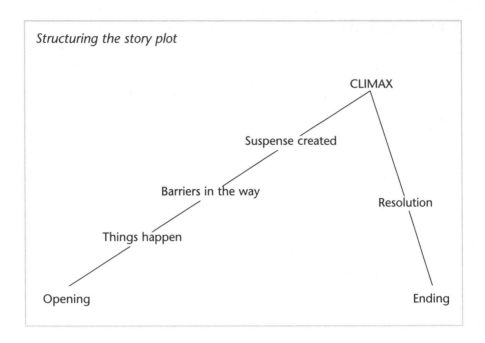

Structuring the story plot

Children can be helped to devise exciting plots for their stories by:

- Analysing plots from stories they have read and asking questions: What is this book about? What are the key events in the story?
- Using the 'what if' question to send the imagination into orbit (what if all the toys come alive at night?).
- Being shown examples of how to place ordinary characters in extraordinary situations or vice versa – girl of today finds herself back in the Viking period; the school secretary looks ordinary enough but she's really a witch.
- Using their own experiences or those they have observed as starting points – divorce, new baby, new pet, growing up and so on.
- Using the idea of cause and consequence as the basis for story structure – one action leads to something else, that leads to...and causes...
- Taking time to plan stories properly, to make the writing easier (more on planning later).

There must be a series of events that happen in sequence and as a result of cause and consequence. For example, in the story about Carole, would the hunk's wife have had an accident if she hadn't been driving too fast? Would she have been driving so fast had she not been upset at finding out that her husband was thinking of moving in with another woman?

Plots also come from life around us. Dependent on age and maturity, children could devise plots from newspaper stories and magazine articles, or they could change the plots from known stories into slightly different ones of their own – add a different ending, change the characters, change the setting or the period.

Creating characters

Characters are the 'who' of stories. Many authors maintain that their plots arise from the characters because real characters will come alive in the story and lead the events that constitute the plot. Let's think about Carole again. If she's a feisty character who thinks mainly of herself, she's not going to let her man go at any price. If she's got a strong conscience, she may encourage him to remain with his wife. But what if she then discovers that she's pregnant? What will she do? Whatever she does advances the plot through the character.

Stories that are written in depth also need to have a range of characters, some to lead the plot and some with minimal 'walk-on' parts, for example, in our 'Carole' story, the policeman who was called to the accident scene. Help children to develop good characterisation by:

- Talking about characters in books they have read – are they good or bad, weak or strong, selfish or thoughtful?

- Describing people – their looks, actions, speech, thoughts etc.

- Cutting out pictures from old magazines and writing about that person, dog, snake, zebra etc.

- Using the 'what if' question: What if the zebra had no stripes? What if that bird couldn't fly?

- Inventing characters with different characteristics to provide the necessary conflict in the story – a go-getter as opposed to a wimp.

- Learning to develop their characters as real and rounded people – ask what that character will do in this or that situation. How will she react to winning the lottery, for example? Will she give some money to charity or spend, spend, spend?

● Thinking about how their characters change throughout the story. If she has won the lottery, how different will her life be and how will her character change as a result?

Obviously characterisation in story writing takes time to develop. At first children tend to write very simply about what happened to someone or something. This happens, then that happens, then something else happens. As they develop their story-sequencing skills, encourage them to let the characters take over and lead the plot. Only then will the characters that children have created become real.

Setting and period

This is the 'where' and 'when' of the story. Stories need to be anchored in particular places and at particular times, whether they are contemporary or historical. When we think about it, if we want our characters to 'live' and become real to us, then their thoughts, actions and responses to others must be reflected against the background of the specific time and place that has shaped them.

Consider the period of a novel set:

● Now – as a contemporary story reflecting 2004.
● In the 1940s.
● In the 1920s or 1930s.
● In Victorian times.

Ask yourself what key events stand out from each period: the Iraqi war, World War II, the General Strike, the inventions and social turmoil that became part of the Industrial Revolution? Many authors specialise in writing regional sagas that centre on a specific area and numerous novels depict human triumph over adversity, often set in the nineteenth and early twentieth centuries.

So, we have established that the period in which the story is set is important, but what about the place? Writers always advise us to write about what we know, but we don't have to have been there to be able to write about it. Many writers rely on their research. Fantasy writers even invent new, often futuristic, places and settings. How can we inspire children to think about settings? We could:

- Present them with a range of settings to choose from – on the beach, on the train, in a space capsule, in a hot-air balloon, on the moon, in the jungle.
- Let them investigate and identify for themselves a range of settings in books they have read.
- Suggest that they move known characters from books they have read into different settings to form a new story – how would the main character in *Rebecca* or Scarlett O'Hara (*Gone with the Wind*) change if their periods and places were reversed? Would the second Mrs de Winter (in *Rebecca*) even survive in Scarlett O'Hara's turbulent world? Can any other two characters be more opposite in their natures?
- Provide those children who need it with some appropriate phrases for expressing time and place in narrative – the next morning, later that evening, back at the den, last month, next year, on the day of my tenth birthday last summer, after Dad had gone to work, and so on. Show children how to use these with the correct verb structures.

I mentioned above that story writing needs to reflect children's own experiences or those of others that they know about. Children's stories could be cross-curricular, for example, set against the background of the ancient Egyptians (history), in France or Spain (linked to modern foreign languages and reflecting the culture of the place), or a village in India (topic in geography). Stories might also reflect some scientific or technological invention. This would help to bring subject work alive as children are encouraged to draw characters from the period or the place.

Hooks and endings

When you are starting a new novel, what makes you want to read on? If the first sentence or paragraph is boring would you bother? The truth is that unless we are buying a book by our favourite author, and trust that author implicitly, the first few paragraphs often influence whether or not we buy a book by a different author. If children are to write good stories that readers want to read, they need to know how to write fiction hooks to get the story going. A fiction hook could be one that immediately, in the first few sentences:

- poses a question;
- opens up a mystery;
- suggests a challenge for the character in the story or the reader.

Let's think about the question words – if, who, why, what, where, when and how – in relation to the following opening lines:

- The footsteps were huge. They could almost be non-human.
- The painting had vanished. But how? It just wasn't possible.
- "Tell me where it is," pleaded Sam.
- "You'll never find it. No one has ever found the golden casket."
- The castle was dark. There was no sound as he approached. Then he heard something… in the undergrowth, behind him.

Opening sentences can also depict or focus on:

- A warning – Don't you dare go down to that forest again!
- A question – Why was the glove left on the table?
- A wish – Why can't I be a fairy? My friend Elspeth is.
- Character – Amanda looked in the mirror and screamed when she saw her green hair.
- Name – I hated my name. Well, how would you like to be called Christmas?
- Drama – The fire started in the attic.
- Time – It was midnight. No moon was out.
- Action – Tom ran faster than he had ever run in his life.

We need to intrigue the reader, to make him/her want to know what the problem is. An opening sentence or paragraph should hint at the conflict around which the plot is based. Children need to study opening lines and paragraphs. They could:

- Sort out the dull ones from the exciting ones.

- Change the dull ones into exciting ones.

- Practise writing single opening lines or short paragraphs and criticise them in pairs or groups.

What about the endings? These should be satisfying to the reader. If enough 'plants' have been placed in the story, the ending should seem natural and plausible because it fits in with what has gone before. For example, if the ending of the story reveals that Amanda is really a fairy disguised as a human, then clues should have been placed throughout the story. For example, earlier in the story, she might have turned up at the party without anyone noticing from the direction of the bottom of the garden. A good ending will also tie up loose ends and reveal to the reader the answers to the questions that have been set up. After all, we all want to know who the killer is when we've been confronted with a murder.

So, as with story openings, present children with lots of different endings to study, talk about and to play around with. Try the following:

- Reflective – John wondered if he would ever go there again.

- Return to the beginning – The ghost laughed, and disappeared through the same door, where Jane had first seen it.

- Twist ending – The secretary was a witch as we had been led to believe, but she was a white witch.

- Final – Father had finally come home to stay.

Variations in sentences

A good story will also include a variety of sentences which perform different roles in the story, for example, to describe a character/setting or to create impact and make the reader stop and think. Sentences should also be of different lengths. Children could experiment with expanding sentences using their knowledge of grammar. Consider how the following sentences have been expanded:

- Run!
- He ran.

- He ran quickly.
- He ran quickly across the field.
- The tramp ran quickly across the field to escape the bull.
- The frightened tramp sprinted quickly across the field to escape the enraged bull.

Try giving children a text written in very short sentences for them to join using conjunctions. They could talk about and give reasons for their choices. If children need support, they could be given some conjunctions to use. Alternatively, if they are able, provide them with long, multi-clause sentences to split up. Talking about the changes is the important learning element of the task. They could also be given a range of words and phrases from which to compose sentences. They will have fun trying to make as many different sentences as they can, by varying the words or by varying the word order, with the same words.

Children also need to study sentences to see what they are doing in the story. Why is that sentence in the form of a question or an exclamation? Also, by collecting and investigating very short sentences, they may conclude that these create tension and impact, while longer sentences slow down the pace and the action of the story, which is why good stories have a balance of both.

It may seem obvious, but work on sentence variations can only be successful with children who have reached the stage of being able to write longer sentences. This is why it is so important to teach all children how to handle sentences so that they can succeed with texts.

Vocabulary for writing

From Year 1, Term 3, the NLS makes continuing references to vocabulary development, in that children 'should make collections of personal interest or significant words and words linked to particular topics'. From Year 2, Term 3, they should be discussing particular types of words and using these to extend and enhance their writing. Throughout primary school there is a strong emphasis on the role that vocabulary development plays in reading and writing.

There is often little time to focus sufficient attention on vocabulary work. Children with inadequate vocabularies struggle to write good fiction because:

- their range of words is limited;
- they stick to the words they know and their vocabulary fails to develop at a pace that sustains the development of writing and spelling;
- lack of vocabulary is a barrier to their learning.

We can help children to be more adventurous writers by developing their vocabularies. Try to:

- Encourage the use of alternative words – offer a range where appropriate.
- Build up vocabulary by oral language activities where possible – every few minutes of focused talk helps.
- Always explain words that are featured in grammar sessions or sentence writing sessions.
- Collect words and sort them into categories according to grammar – nouns, verbs and so on.
- Sort words according to categories of meaning – for example, words of colour, size and shape, or words to describe people, animals, plants.
- Teach children how to use a thesaurus when they are ready.
- Use paired and group sessions to talk about words in the context of sentences.
- Use cloze activities (filling in gaps with missing words or phrases) – the children can do this in pairs or groups, talking about the different effects created and the 'best' words for the spaces (see box below).
- Bring in objects for children to describe.
- Give the children a 'feely' bag and ask them to describe the objects in it by the 'feel' only.
- Use the senses – describe sounds and smells, as well as what we see and feel.
- Encourage children to take risks and praise any attempts at using adventurous vocabulary in speech and writing.

Examples of cloze activities

How many words can you find to fit each space? Which is the best? When designing a 'missing word' activity, try leaving out particular words – nouns, adjectives or verbs. You could leave out phrases too.

Mum went to the . . .
King John was a . . . king.
The lion . . . on his prey.

How does vocabulary affect sentence writing? Think of the difference between a black and white and a colour television. Well-chosen vocabulary adds colour to all fiction. Children should check that their choice of words is right for a particular text in terms of:

● Grammar – is an adjective/noun/adverb right in this space?
● Meaning – does this word make sense?
● Effect upon the reader – will it create the emotion that I want the reader to feel?

Consider the following sentence:

The pretty dog strolled across the room.

Is the word 'pretty' the right word to describe a dog? It is an adjective, so it fits grammatically, but it is hardly a suitable adjective to describe that particular noun. Does a dog stroll? Dogs run, bound, scamper, jump, bolt, sprint and possibly amble, but they do not stroll. Children could be encouraged to explore the effect of using different words in a particular text. They could also collect words that match particular genres of fiction. Consider the words and phrases listed below:

Vocabulary needs to fit the genre

flowers / perfume / body / blood / murder / gun / smile / table in a restaurant / gift-wrapped / soft and gentle / eyes as cold as ice / a locked door / love / a flickering glow / white silk / cold steel
Which might suggest mystery or crime and which could suggest romance?

Structuring longer pieces of writing

One of the problems that children experience when writing stories is being unable to hold onto longer pieces. Some writers lose their thread halfway down the page and ramble on, often going nowhere. The story then loses any shape and structure. Sometimes this can be addressed by more effective planning (more on this in Chapter 7), but often the writer simply gets carried away part-way through and loses track.

Try showing children how to:

- Write in paragraphs – one paragraph should encompass one idea. Give the children a set of mixed sentences to sort into paragraphs that make up a story (see box below) – for example, some might be about the weather, some might describe the character, some may belong to a different timeframe and so on.

- Use **narrative links** in stories, for example, to show the passage of time – several weeks passed, this time, the next day. Highlight narrative links in texts that children have read and analyse how they move the story on.

- Cut up paragraphs from known stories for children to put in the right order.

- Discuss the clues they used to decide on the sequence of each paragraph – which were the key words?

- Use prediction – when we ask children to predict what might happen next we are asking them to focus on the expected structure of the story.

- Compose a group story – each child to provide a paragraph (having talked about the plot first), then talk about how well each paragraph fits together.

● Focus on the type of story it is, and where it is going – this may help to keep children's minds on track.

Sorting sentences into paragraphs

She wore a lovely green dress. It was raining heavily. The dog scampered down the road. It matched her eyes beautifully. Everything was soaked. The butcher's shop door was open. Even the papers were dripping. The sausages were too tempting. Jealousy is not a pretty sight. The butcher was not quick enough. The ink ran down in rivulets. The dog sprinted out of the shop with a long line of sausages trailing behind.

In addition we could help children to think about the coherence of longer pieces by thinking about aspects of comprehension, using books they have read and their own writing. Children could be shown how to:

● Summarise the main idea of each paragraph in just a few words, and to ask: 'What is this paragraph about? Does this paragraph lead on from the last one? What should the next paragraph be about?'

● Track the causes and consequences of events in the story – do they fit together logically?

● Analyse the sequence of key events in the plot as the skeleton of the story: What are these key events? Do they contribute to the overall structure of beginning, middle and end?

● Write a **blurb** for a story – this is the text printed at the front or back of a book to 'sell' it to readers.

● Write a **synopsis** and stick to the main points.

● Recognise other aspects of story writing that put the flesh upon the skeleton and that these details give the story colour, depth, dimension and readability – for example, the choice of vocabulary, the variations in sentences or the use of dialogue.

Writing playscripts

The NLS framework introduces children to playscripts through reading and acting out plays early on, but not until Year 3 do the NLS objectives refer explicitly to writing playscripts. Consider the list below.

NLS objectives for writing playscripts

Year 3, Term 1	To read, prepare and present playscripts.
Year 4, Term 1	To write playscripts using known stories as a basis.
Year 5, Term 2	To write own playscripts applying the conventions learned from reading, including production notes.
Year 5, Term 2	To evaluate scripts and performance for dramatic interest and impact.

From the Foundation Stage, children should have experienced some drama. They will have taken part in role play and imagined themselves as doctors, dentists or travel agents according to the changing focus of the role-play corner. Many children will also have been introduced to plays at the theatre or on TV, so by the time they are required to write plays, the notion of what a playscript is should not be totally alien.

Both stories and playscripts are works of fiction. But while conventional narrative tells the story through a balance of prose and dialogue, plays have to reveal the whole story through dialogue. Both genres must have a strong narrative structure. Plays have a beginning, middle and end, just as conventional stories, and the points made above with reference to story writing are equally applicable to plays.

To write plays, children must be able to write dialogue that does many jobs. That dialogue must be brilliant at multi-tasking! It should:

- Tell the story by moving the plot forward.
- Tell the reader about the characters and develop the characterisation as the play moves along.
- Deliver the intrigue, empathy, effect and depth of emotion in the same way as conventional stories.

Playscripts do, of course, have a narrator to help set the scene and tell the actors how to say their lines. Assuming that children have read a number of playscripts and have already transformed some known stories into playscript format, we can further develop their knowledge and skills by:

- Modelling the written conventions of playscripts (see box below).
- Helping them to choose characters that are different and distinctive but few in number – films often include hundreds of extras but in plays the number of characters should be restricted.
- Helping them to write dialogue that matches each character as the play depends on this. It will not work if all the characters speak in the same way. Would an Oxford professor speak like a Glasgow bus driver?
- Collaborative play writing – have fun with children each inventing a character and weaving their character through a group-based plot. Such activities also help to develop group social skills.

Written conventions of playscripts

Write the character's name.
Put the stage directions in brackets.
Write each new speaker's words on a new line.
There is no need to use 'he said'.
There is no need for speech marks.

Example

Mr Mad (angrily waving his pen): Get out from under that table!
John (softly): I'm stuck, Sir.
Mr Mad: I'll give you five seconds . . . one, two . . .

Many of the activities that are suggested for stories can help to develop playwriting. Ensure that the children keep the structure of the play under control as using dialogue alone makes it easier to stray off-track. The playscripts that children are required to write can at least rely on props and costumes. Think how much more difficult it must be to write a play for radio with the sole emphasis on listening.

Writing poetry

Poetry is a valuable part of literacy, and poetry texts are particularly useful for supporting the word level requirements of the NLS framework. Consider the NLS objectives listed below as a starting point to our brief exploration of poetry writing.

Example NLS objectives for writing poetry

Year 1, Term 1	To use rhymes and patterned stories as models for own writing.
Year 2, Term 1	To use simple poetry structures . . . substitute own ideas.
Year 2, Term 3	To use humorous verse.
Year 4, Term 1	To write poetry that uses sound to create effects.
Year 5, Term 1	To write poems, experimenting with different styles and structures.

From the Foundation Stage, children will have been playing and experimenting with rhyme to develop their phonological awareness, all of which supports poetry. But children need to be taught that poetry, as opposed to verse, is not just about rhyme.

How would you describe a poem? The aim of writing poetry is to get children to use language expressively. Poems offer opportunities for children to communicate their thoughts, feelings and ideas in an intensive written form. Poetry work could be seen as a language development opportunity within a creative context. Poems could also be regarded as creating pictures from words.

The purpose of this section is not to discuss different types of poems, but to explore some of the main points that may help children to enjoy writing poetry. There are many reasons why children may enjoy writing poetry more than other forms of writing, for example:

● Poetry is short – less able or reluctant writers often welcome this.

● There is less emphasis on grammar.

- Poetry can allow writers to show emotion and feelings about themselves, key issues, nature and so on.
- Poetry can be a therapeutic activity.

So what aspects of writing poetry do children need to know? The modelling and experimentation with poems during shared reading and writing will take into account different forms of poetry, but we could also help children to think about:

- Colourful vocabulary – poetry seeks to evoke strong images, so make words specific (not just cat, but Siamese).
- Powerful nouns and verbs that create strong pictures rather than overloading with adjectives and adverbs.
- The theme of the poem – what is the main idea? Ask children to jot down as many words as they can around given themes.
- Sound – as they read their poems aloud to get the rhythm and beat just like music.
- Shape – all poems have a shape that is often dictated by the type of poem. Show children models of the different shapes.
- **Similes** and **metaphors**.
- Phrases for poems based on meaning-carrying words with as few function words as possible.
- Creating word pictures.

Make sure that children know how poetry writing is different from story writing. I can recall many children who, having spent much time on sentence writing, struggled to grasp the fact that sentences and full stops do not feature in poems in the same way as other text level work.

Many children find it difficult to write in the abbreviated and economical style of a poem. If you think about it, they have mentally to discard many of the rules they have been taught in the context of good writing, for example, grammar. Encourage children to be adventurous and to throw caution to the wind when writing poetry. They need to take risks, to invent and to see what works. A poem works if it has an effect upon the reader. Just like other writing, poetry needs to be worked on and redrafted. Reading poems aloud will help this process.

Also encourage children to carry on without stopping once they have begun to write a poem. They don't have to worry about spelling, sentences or full stops. The words and phrases that surround the initial idea should spill out onto the page (or keyboard) without interruption. Only then should the redrafting and shaping begin as the pieces are moved around to get the best fit.

Finally, what could children write poems about? Ideas might come from:

● Family issues – exploring feelings and emotions.
● Funny things that have happened to them.
● Things brought into school – pictures, objects, artefacts for history, toys.
● Work done across the curriculum – a poem about the Romans, in the jungle etc.
● What they love or hate.
● Dreams and aspirations.
● Their special memories.
● News stories they have come across.

You might want children to reflect on the things in life that often go unnoticed, for example, the rain, a smile, a tree, a kind thought.

The children will have plenty of their own ideas for poems and will be better motivated to write about their own themes than those prescribed by adults. Encourage them to write poetry for themselves as well as for others. Most text level writing is for other audiences, but poetry, like writing a diary, can be personal. Having a small notebook handy and being encouraged to write a poem regularly can be therapeutic for some children.

Of course, poetry needs to be redrafted and presented with as much care as other forms of writing, if for an audience. For me, poems have a dual purpose. They need not always be profound or reflective – some can be light-hearted and funny. Poems should say as much as possible in as few words as possible. We are creating word pictures, so vocabulary has to be colourful, not bland, as each word has to work hard. Poems, unlike stories or plays, do only present the skeleton. They are also about language patterns. How do the language patterns work for each of the poems in the box below?

Poem ideas

Sounds
The whisper of the wind in the night
The chatter of voices at a barbecue
The crunch of a crisp bag as you put it in the bin
The ping of the microwave when the potato's ready
The screams of people as the bomb goes off

My sister	*I like*
Likes muesli	Porridge with hot milk
Goes out on her bike	Crumpets with strawberry jam
Wears red and orange	Toast with melted butter
Loses her temper	Sausages with baked beans

Shape poem – snakes
Snakes with slender bodies
                slither slowly
                        slink and slide
                                curl and hide

All children can write poems – even those who think they are not good writers – and poems can help to give children confidence because they are never 'right or wrong'. Poems can be personal or they can be shared. Children could write collaboratively on a jointly agreed theme.

The Resources section includes further reading on fiction for those who wish to extend their skills and knowledge.

Summary

In this chapter I have looked at:

- Some of the key points for writing stories, playscripts and poetry. Text level work is complex and many children will find aspects difficult as the work progresses. This does not imply that such children are necessarily 'poor writers' or that they 'can't write'. Ways can always be found to make writing tasks easier for children who struggle (dealing with difficulties is discussed in Chapter 7).

Chapter 6

Writing at text level: non-fiction

Most of the key strategies for helping children to write at text level have been included in the previous chapter. This chapter explores the characteristics of non-fiction writing and includes:

● Explanations and examples of different text types and their format.
● Suggestions for supporting children's skills in writing non-fiction.
● Dealing with diagrammatic format.

What is a non-fiction text?

What constitutes your own reading and writing? This is something we rarely think about, yet we are involved in helping children to read and write at text level in preparation for what they will read and write *as adults*. You could try making a list of the non-fiction texts you have read or written this week or month. The box below lists examples of the range of text types most adults come across as part of their normal reading or writing.

List of common non-fiction texts		
Diary	Book on DIY	Newspaper
Telephone directory	Menu	Magazine
Train timetable	Fire instructions	Labels
Bus timetable	Leaflet	Advertisements
Post-redirection form	TV listings	Cinema/theatre listings etc.
Note to the milkman	Letter to a friend	Report
Shopping list		

Your list will no doubt include different examples, but both indicate the range of texts most adults read. It has been established that the majority of what is read and written by adults constitutes non-fiction, and that children need support if they are to get to grips with the range and format of these types of texts.

Reflecting adult non-fiction – purpose, audience and format

Clearly we can't teach children how to write non-fiction solely through adult texts – we need texts at child level that reflect adult writing. Consider the NLS objectives that guide work on non-fiction in the primary school. These give us some idea of what children are expected to achieve.

NLS objectives for non-fiction texts	
Year 1, Term 2	To make simple lists for planning and reminding. To write simple instructions and labels.
Year 2, Term 2	To use diagrams in instructions. To use appropriate register in writing instructions – direct, impersonal.
Year 2, Term 3	Produce simple flowcharts that explain a process. Make simple notes from non-fiction texts. To write non-chronological reports.
Year 4, Term 1	To write letters, notes and messages. Experiment with recounting the same event in a variety of ways (e.g. story, letter, newspaper report).
Year 4, Term 2	To write newspaper-style reports.
Year 4, Term 3	To fill out brief notes into connected prose.
Year 5, Term 1	To present a point of view in writing. To summarise key ideas. To design an advert.
Year 6, Term 3	Revise language conventions and grammatical features of different types of texts – narrative, recounts, instructions, reports, explanations, persuasive, discursive texts.

The expectations are high and many children will struggle to achieve all of the objectives listed above by the end of Year 6. Much of the work on non-fiction will take place in the literacy hour, but a significant proportion needs to happen *in other subjects*.

The principles for writing outlined in Chapter 2 also apply to non-fiction. The box below outlines the range of purpose, audience and format that guides our thinking when writing a non-fiction text. Imagine the possible computations! No wonder it's difficult, for adults as well as learners.

Purpose, audience and format

Purpose	**Audience**	**Format**
To provide information	Ourselves	Labels
To record information	One other child	Graphs
For discussion	Another class	List
For amusement	Family members	Flowchart
To persuade (advert)	Unknown readership	Matrix
To report	Friend	Pie graph
To explain how something works	The boss	Bar chart
To communicate (memo)		
To instruct		
To question		

For what purpose might the following texts be written?

- A recount of the school trip to York Museum.
- Labels for the new school cupboards.
- Instructions for operating the new computer.
- Note to the school secretary.
- Note to the school gardener stating what flowers the class would like him to plant.
- Letter to the 'crisps' company complaining about the quality of the latest batch.
- Notice for the school jumble sale or craft fair.

- Letter to the school dinner ladies to apologise for being cheeky during the lunch break.

We can identify a real purpose for *most* of the texts that children are required to write, apart perhaps from writing sessions that aim to practise parts of texts. If we are to emulate adult non-fiction in school, we need to identify the types of writing used regularly in subjects other than the literacy hour and any extended English work. You might want to list some cross-curricular writing with which you are familiar. In general, your list probably reflects some of mine:

Being creative through cross-curricular writing

Science	Writing up the results of an experiment.
History	Writing a newspaper report of a battle.
	Writing a poem based on the events of World War I or conditions in the city slums at the time of the Industrial Revolution.
Geography	Bar chart of climate or weather for a particular country.
Art	Venn diagram to show how colours combine to form others.
Maths	A range of number and data work – bar charts, pie charts, graphs, flowcharts.
Design and technology	Instructions for making a model of a Tudor house.
Music	Writing the music itself or responding in writing to music that is heard.

We could also vary the writing tasks for a single theme – for example, class writing that emanates from work on the Battle of Hastings could be presented in many different formats as shown below. This is also one way to differentiate writing for different levels of ability and interests.

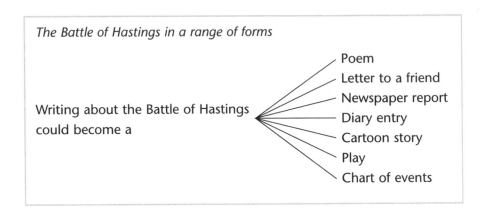

The Battle of Hastings in a range of forms

Writing about the Battle of Hastings could become a

- Poem
- Letter to a friend
- Newspaper report
- Diary entry
- Cartoon story
- Play
- Chart of events

Even translating non-fiction into fiction style is a positive activity as it helps to reinforce the notion of fiction, non-fiction and 'faction' (real events written up in a fiction style). Let's now look at the significant features of each main text type.

▧ **Considering text types**

When writing different text types, our thoughts are guided by four basic considerations:

- Purpose
- Audience
- Format
- Use of language

In general, the purpose and the audience dictate the format and the use of the language. For example, if the purpose is to write a letter to Mum who is away on a training course, the format would be that of a letter and the language would be informal. If the purpose is to write a report, the format would be more structured and language more formal.

Recount

- Purpose – to retell an event or something that has happened, often focusing on specific occasions or people.

- Audience may be known or general.
- Often chronological – the events are recounted in sequential order: We went to the museum, then we had a coffee, next we ... finally, we ...
- Often past tense verbs – I visited, we went, we enjoyed.
- Common use of first person – 'I' and 'we'.
- Sequential words to denote chronological nature of text – *next, then, after that.*

Report

- Purpose – to describe how things are, the type of information we would expect to read in a non-fiction book:
  - All about sharks
  - The tourist in Japan
  - Class 1C in 2004.
- Often written for an unknown, general readership.
- Conventional sentence structure; depending on the level of formality, the writer may use the passive voice.
- Often describes the generic properties or features of things:
  - Sharks are dangerous. There are many different species of shark.
  - Japan has a population of ... The capital city is Tokyo.
  - There are 32 children in class 1C. 56% are girls. The rest are boys.

Explanation

- Purpose – to explain how something works or the processes involved. Explanations often answer questions such as 'how?' or 'why?':
  - How do plants grow?
  - Why do we have day and night?
- Written for a general readership.
- Often has an opening statement to introduce the topic to be explained.
- Is followed by a series of logical steps or descriptions.
- May have diagrams to support the text.

- May use present or past tense, and passive verb structure.
- Often focuses on 'cause and effect' – because of this, consequently, as a result.

Argument

- Purpose – to present a point of view on an issue:
  - Fox hunting should be banned.
  - We should not have to wear school uniform.
- Often for presentation to a known audience or may be a general readership.
- Often has an opening statement to open the case and give the writer's point of view:
  - We should not have to wear school uniform.
- Is followed by points to support the argument, often in the present tense:
  - School uniform inhibits people's individuality.
  - Some parents may not be able to afford it.
- Usually has a closing definitive statement – for example:
  - For these reasons, I believe that school uniform should be abolished.

Discussion

- Purpose – to open up a debate on an issue, to present a balanced argument like an essay but not as strongly as for an argument. A discussion text presents opposing points of view for the reader to consider:
  - Should we have school uniform?
- Opens with a statement to introduce the issue.
- Continues with the rationale for both sides of the issue.
- May have a final summary or conclusion that often leaves the reader to decide which 'side' he/she is on.
- Presented mainly for a non-specific, general readership.
- Language used may be like that of an argument with use of logical connectives – however, therefore, because, in this case.

Procedure or instructional

- Purpose – how to make or to do things:
  - How to make your own Christmas crackers.
  - Directions for the bus station.
  - How to bake a sponge cake.
- Is in sequential order:
  - First assemble your ingredients.
  - Turn the oven to gas mark 6/200°C.
  - Cream the sugar and margarine.
- Often states what you will need if the instruction is to do a job or to make something.
- Each part of the instruction often starts with the verb.
- Strong emphasis on telling the reader what to do.
- May have diagrams to support the instructions.

Persuasion

- Purpose – to persuade you to do or to buy something (e.g. advert or promotional literature for loans or private health insurance).
- Opening statement or question to gain your interest:
  - What could you do with five thousand pounds?
- Followed by reasons why you should buy the product or do whatever is suggested – for example, comparisons with other loan companies.
- Use of simple present tense and logical connectives.

There are six basic text types, but I have separated an argument from a discussion. It is important to remember that few texts fall into one distinct category – a persuasive text and an argument are also similar in purpose. I often think of persuasive texts as those in the form of adverts or promotional leaflets. Consider the text examples in the box below. How would you classify each one?

Which text types are these?

1   A holiday brochure.
2   A map to help you to find your way round the museum.
3   A leaflet advertising a loan.
4   Information from the bank on new interest rates or a new customer account.
5   An article in a magazine about how mobile phones work.
6   A notice about the church jumble sale.
7   Article on 'Climbing in the French Alps' in *Exotic Places* magazine.
8   A menu in a restaurant.
9   Recipes in a cookery book.
10 Article entitled 'Should our water be chlorinated?' in a magazine.

Not all of the texts you may classify as one type necessarily use the same structure or style of language. Much depends on the writer and *how he/she wants to communicate with the readership.* This is the essence of what we want to convey to children. The design of non-fiction texts is all to do with purpose and audience. It's far from easy. Some texts listed above are more obvious, for example numbers 2 and 9 are instructional, while numbers 1, 3, 4 and 6 are persuasive in different ways. At the same time, these persuasive texts offer information to help you to make up your mind, for example, the leaflet from the bank on its new interest rates may also contain a report section on how well their assets have recently performed. Number 10 is clearly a discussion article on the points for and against chlorinating our water, while number 5 is an explanation. Did you think of number 7 as a recount, assuming that it is describing the enjoyable holiday experience of the writer? Yet, such articles often point out the many benefits of going to such exotic places and are *persuading* you, albeit implicitly, to go there and enjoy similar experiences.

Let's think about the children. What kinds of writing from a range of subject areas might emulate some of the text types we have been exploring? Consider the list below – you may like to add some more of your own.

Non-fiction writing in school

1 A recipe for chocolate caramel cookies in the school magazine.
2 A discussion piece: 'Was Queen Victoria a good or a bad queen?'
3 An evaluation of the class design and technology project.
4 An article on the life of Van Gogh.
5 Piece on 'How I survived in the jungle'.
6 Children in Key Stage 2 writing a book on 'Sharks' for children in Key Stage 1.
7 A report on the school trip for the school magazine.
8 Information for parents on which writing/spelling objectives are being focused on this term.
9 Rules on 'How to behave in the school dining room'.

There is no reason why children, in groups or as individuals, cannot be involved in writing texts such as those above (even that suggested in number 8).

Supporting non-fiction writing

To support children's non-fiction writing we need to help them with the design of particular texts and the processes involved in writing a range of texts.

Designing a text

I've suggested constantly throughout this book that writing is thinking – what we do with our brains is just as important as what we subsequently do on paper or on the keyboard. So to help children to design non-fiction texts we need to work on the answers to the following questions with them:

● The purpose – why am I writing this?
● Who are my readers and how do I want them to respond?
● Do I need some diagrams to support the writing?

- What structure does my text need to have – chronological or does it not matter?
- What kind of language do I need to use – community and chatty or strictly SE and formal?
- Should I use the first person (I and we) or the third person (he, they)?
- Should I use the active or the passive voice?

Supporting the processes of writing non-fiction texts

Once children have talked through the answers to these questions with an adult, they should have identified clearly what text type they need to write and be ready to plan and write their non-fiction text. The answers to the above questions may also identify where the next set of problems lie, as many children will need explicit help with the writing itself.

The main problems that will emerge during work on non-fiction writing are likely to be those of structure at sentence and text level, as there will be many children – perhaps those who have some degree of learning difficulty or for whom English is an additional language – who will find particular difficulties with structuring non-fiction texts. We can support the processes of writing at **text level** by:

- Modelling the particular text type that is needed.
- Pointing out its main characteristics (highlighting these if possible).
- Helping the child to use the main characteristics in his/her own text.
- Providing a writing frame as a scaffold (see next chapter).
- Responding to the first draft with constructive and uplifting comments.
- Encouraging children to redraft using the model as a guide.

Of course, prior to the work on particular texts, and taking place alongside it, children must develop a general notion of what non-fiction is about. They could begin by collecting examples of different texts from:

- Work done across the curriculum – examples from different subject areas.
- Home – examples from postal deliveries.

- Around the locality – what is available in shops, supermarkets, the dentist's surgery and so on.

Over time, the range of texts collected could be extensively discussed (good use of group talk as children debate which text belongs where), categorised, labelled and stored, to provide models for when they are needed. Some of these text examples could also become writing frames.

At **sentence level**, we may need to support the writing process by providing:

- Examples of sentences using different viewpoints (first or third person).
- Examples of active and passive verb structures.
- Examples of phrases to suit that particular text type.

At **word level**, we may need to support the process further by providing:

- Stock words or phrases for a particular type of text, for example, the verbs for instructional texts.
- Specialised vocabulary, for example, to suit the type of readership.

Making and rebuilding notes

In order to use information from non-fiction texts we often have to take notes. You may recently have taken notes from:

- Listening to a speaker on a training course.
- A book that you used to obtain information.
- A staff meeting.

Why did you make your notes? Was it to rebuild them into prose again? Was it to remind yourself of the key points and help these to stay in your memory? What bits of information did you particularly want to know about? What was your *purpose*? Whatever the reason, the main skill in note-taking is to sift out the main meaning-carrying words from the other mainly functional words that have the least meaning. Consider the examples of notes below. Which do you think are the more effective?

Examples of notes

1 Everyone knows – the loud trumpeting sound that elephants make – make this noise when they are excited, surprised, angry or lost. Their low rumbles might mean 'Where are you?' Females signal when they are ready – and warn each other of danger. Elephants also make visual displays – they move their ears and trunks – stand tall – raise its trunk, shake its head, flap its ears.

2 Elephants – trumpeting sound when surprised, excited, angry, lost. Low rumbles = where are you? Females signal – to mate. Warn of danger. Touch and smell. Perform visual displays – move ears, trunk, stand tall to increase threat, raise trunk, flap ears, shake head.

You may have picked out number 2 as the more economical, with determiners mainly left out. In school, children may have to take notes in the following ways:

- Listening to the teacher or supporting adult and jotting down key points.
- Taking notes from a book to build up later for a 'finding out' project.
- Taking notes for homework tasks.

Without a clear purpose children may miss important information hidden within a text or in speech. They need to ask questions such as:

- 'What do I already know about this topic?'
- 'What do I need to find out?'

We can help children to develop effective note-making skills by:

- Training them to identify their purpose and ask their own questions before they start to make notes.
- Modelling examples of effective notes and talking about why they are effective.
- Making it clear to children that notes are not written as sentences – tell them to forget about sentences and focus on meaning-carrying words.
- Summarising the main idea of chapters and paragraphs to get children to extract the main ideas from those that merely support.

- Highlighting from texts the words that we might take as notes and comparing these in small groups – why has this word been noted as opposed to that one?
- Giving children copies of the same set of notes to build up into prose and comparing the different outcomes.

Remember that some children, especially those with language difficulties, will have immense problems with note-taking, particularly at speed. They may not be able to:

- Process what is heard (from speech) in order to choose the right words.
- Sift out the main meaning-carrying words from the sea of language that is washing over them (listening comprehension).
- Write down their notes fast enough (handwriting problems).
- Separate the main ideas of what they read from those that merely support (reading comprehension problems).
- Build up prose from their notes as these are likely to be inefficient.

All we can do is to make the task as accessible as possible and offer practice sessions that train children to pay attention to the key points above. Try to:

- Stress the meaning-carrying words when giving verbal note-taking practice.
- Give short dictation at speed to encourage children to listen and write as quickly as possible – for many children speed is the main problem.
- Use word cards – the children can sort the meaning-carrying words from the functional words.
- Relate notes to some of the points made about poetry to encourage children to sift out the most effective words. Like poetry, note-taking uses language economically.

Think about note-taking from the perspective of reading comprehension. It may seem obvious, but we can't make effective notes unless we have fully understood the information we have listened to or read. Our notes will often reflect an aspect of language within the text that stems from our reading comprehension. For example, we may have perceived that a sentence or paragraph focuses on:

- A main idea – essential to the note-making, the idea that recapitulates the text.

- Supporting details – some important, others not.

- Cause and effect – why something happened and the consequences.

- Comparison between people or things – for example, between the Romans and the Vikings in a history book.

- Sequence – order being important to the understanding of the text.

Direct children's attention to these aspects of comprehension that are implicit within the language, as these, alongside the purpose for taking notes, guide the choice of words and phrases.

Dealing with diagrammatic information

Non-fiction texts may need to include a diagram. But what form of diagram would be best for that particular text? This is a key question that children need to ask as part of their text design. Many different diagrams appear within non-fiction texts but here are some examples of how information might be presented.

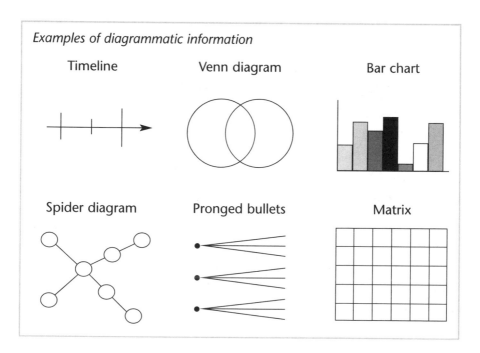

Examples of diagrammatic information

Timeline Venn diagram Bar chart

Spider diagram Pronged bullets Matrix

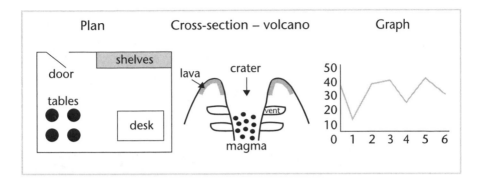

We also use diagrams as a form of notes when planning and organising information prior to writing. Which type of diagram would you choose for each of the text types, as notes or to accompany the text? We might choose a timeline to organise information for recount writing or for instructions, to reflect the chronological nature of the data. Or note cards could be placed on a washing line in sequential order. A Venn or a spider diagram may be more suitable for non-chronological report writing, while for an explanation, we may decide to include a cross-section.

The pronged bullet type of diagram may be best for persuasive writing in order to link the main points with the supporting evidence. For a discussion text we might want to use a diagram that enhances the comparative 'either…or' aspect of such a text, for example, columns to show 'for and against'.

By looking at the different leaflets and notices around us we can see how diagrammatic format is used to enhance the impact of each text by directing the reader's thought processes, perhaps towards comparison (two columns), sequence (timeline), or cause and effect (spider diagram). Only by experiencing the range of diagrammatically presented information from the locality and from different areas of the curriculum can children gradually learn how to use these within their own non-fiction texts or as efficient note-taking devices. We can help by:

- Collecting examples of texts with different diagrams.
- Talking about the information presented.
- Talking about why that diagram has been chosen to represent that particular piece of information – why would a different type of diagram not be better?

Non-fiction texts are possibly more difficult for children to get to grips with than fiction. After all, children are introduced to stories virtually from babyhood. Non-fiction is also more complex and demands a sound understanding of Standard English, with a level of vocabulary from which to select the appropriate words. For some children, some non-fiction words and phrases need to be specifically taught.

Summary

In this chapter I have looked at:

- The range of non-fiction text types.
- Their characteristics.
- Note-making and the use of diagrams as part of texts.
- Strategies to support children's non-fiction writing.

Chapter 7

Planning, redrafting and dealing with difficulties

Writing is thinking. Few writers (beginners or professionals) actually start their text from a blank page without some kind of planning. The planning facilitates the writing and helps to keep it on track. Redrafting is also essential if the finished product is to be fit for its intended audience. At text level, the first draft rarely communicates what any writer intends – most writers have to work at writing as a craft. It is hard slog! Of course, we don't want children to perceive writing as a hard slog, but we do want them to take a pride in their achievements and to appreciate the importance of redrafting when it matters. Having gone through the complexities of writing fiction and non-fiction, we can also understand why some children struggle to write anything at all.

This chapter offers suggestions for:

- Sharing and scaffolding the writing process for children.
- Helping children to plan writing.
- Helping children to redraft writing.
- Dealing with significant writing difficulties.

Sharing and scaffolding the writing process

If you are required to lead or support a shared/guided writing session, this section provides some useful suggestions.

Shared writing

The aim of shared reading and writing is for the adult and the children to share a text together. The role of the adult is to:

- Model the text to be focused on.
- Explain its key characteristics – what type of genre, its main features, what is special about it, and why the text is set out in a particular way.
- Lead collaborative composition modelled on the text shown.

Together, children and adults:

- Establish an *audience* and a *purpose* for the writing.
- Talk about how this determines the *structure* and the *grammatical elements* of the particular piece.

In Reception and Year 1, this may be limited in extent – a list, a rhyme, a caption, a brief account of a school visit or a simple character description. In Key Stage 2, shared writing needs to take on more sophisticated dimensions as the texts worked on become longer and more complex. It is difficult to engage all children's attention during a shared writing session, but the following ideas may help:

- Try to arrange sharply focused (two-minute) talk sessions in pairs – to decide on the 'best' word to fit a space or to discuss a point made.
- Children could hold up response cards, for example, during grammar work, each card could illustrate a 'verb', 'noun' or 'adjective' etc. Children hold up the correct card when a word in the text is said or shown.
- Stress key vocabulary or use a picture to help to fix new words in children's minds.
- Keep them alert – occasionally make deliberate errors for them to put right.
- Check for misunderstandings and try to deal with them, but without losing the pace of the session too much.
- Try to balance listening, speaking, reading and writing interactively, for example, children may be listening to the adult and reading for a few

minutes as they absorb information about a text. They might then write a response on a white board, followed by talking to a partner about what they've written.

- Stick closely to the objectives – it is easy to wander off-track, especially when children ask questions or make comments that are not relevant to the focus of the session. Irrelevant but important issues could be followed up later.

Guided writing and scaffolding

Guided writing differs from shared writing as children move from modelling, discussion about texts and shared composition, to the task of writing under controlled conditions. This is often called scaffolding. 'Help me do it' is something learners often say as they take their first faltering steps. Whether the task is learning to walk, ride a bicycle or swim, 'in none of these cases can the learner simply move completely from observing to performing' (Wray 2002).

During the guided writing, children are usually grouped by ability so that the adult can:

- Guide each child's efforts and make suggestions that will lead the writing forward.
- Put right any misconceptions noticed.
- Give children the individual attention that is not so easy to provide in whole classes.

Using a writing frame

Writing frames act as a scaffold to 'cushion' children between the shared and the independent experiences. A writing frame should do exactly what it is supposed to do, and needs to be appropriate for each learner's level of development. The frame takes away the frightening effect of the 'blank page' and offers some security as a starting point. Writing frames can be used to guide both fiction and non-fiction by providing a skeleton outline of the text. Their purpose is to enable independence. Therefore children may need different levels of 'framing'. For example:

- More skilled writers may only need prompts – a few starter words or brief notes in order for them to begin work independently.
- Less skilled writers may need their frame to include a model of how a text is set out from which they can copy.
- Some children with special educational needs may need a more cushioned type of frame with much of the writing already done – perhaps with words, sentences or paragraphs to be filled in.

See the examples of writing frames below.

A minimal writing frame (some pupils may need only odd words)

1 For a recount – museum, time, what we learned, what we saw.
2 About elephants – habitat, food, how they live, communication.

A more structured writing frame (to prompt the writer's thoughts)

1 I enjoyed our visit to the museum because...
   We went to see the...
   After that we...
   Before we got back onto the coach we visited...
   My most exciting part of the visit was...

2 The frame could be in the form of a 'fact tree'.

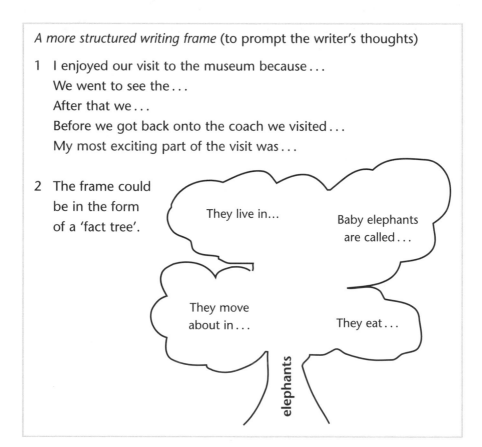

Planning to write

Consider some objectives from the NLS framework that focus on planning listed below.

> *NLS objectives for planning*
>
> **Year 1, Term 2**   To make simple lists for planning and reminding.
> **Year 3, Term 1**   To generate ideas relevant to a topic.
> **Year 3, Term 2**   To plan main points as a structure for story writing.
>   To describe and sequence key incidents in a variety
>   of ways – charting, mapping, storyboards.
> **Year 4, Term 1**   Use different ways of planning stories.

If we ask children what writing is, rarely will they mention listening, talking or thinking. Let's consider some models for planning fiction and non-fiction.

Brain showering

The purpose of this is to extract information quickly from the brain by exploring what we already have 'filed away'. In a sense, this can be an act of rediscovery as we realise, often to our surprise, that we know more than we think we do. Explore your brain! Expand on the following topics and see where your thoughts lead you:

- Fish
- Water
- Berlin
- The moon

Sometimes many brains work better than one – collaborative planning works well at all levels.

Spider diagrams

Consider the example below. Ask children to start off with one 'magnet' word and then produce a word web around it.

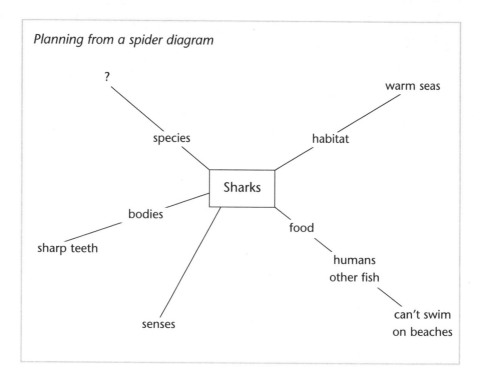

Planning from a spider diagram

?

species

warm seas

habitat

Sharks

bodies

sharp teeth

food

humans
other fish

can't swim
on beaches

senses

Start from an object and let the ideas grow

The longer we look at something, the more thoughts flood the mind. In the bath I stared at the sponge I had bought from Symi and dredged up distant memories of Greek Islands, the talk on diving for sponges, the dangers of the 'bends' and so on.

Draw a grid to represent sections or chapters of text level work

For fiction this is often called a storyboard.

Planning from a grid		
Amanda meets fairy	Fairy takes her to visit Fairyland	Amanda lives just like a fairy for a day
Chief fairy wants Amanda to stay with them for ever	?	?

Listing to generate ideas

Simply ask pupils to produce 10 (or 5 or 20) words or phrases around a given topic in five minutes.

Listing key events on a flowchart

Consider the example below as a way of organising the main events in a story or a play.

Flowchart for key events
1 Jenny wins a holiday as a prize in a competition.
2 While on the holiday she meets Jack and strikes up a friendship.
3 Jack mysteriously disappears.
4 Jenny goes off on a quest to find him and so on.

Journey mapping

Map out the sequence of a story or a non-fiction piece like the example below. It's a bit like a map of the Underground with the 'stations' along the route as key events.

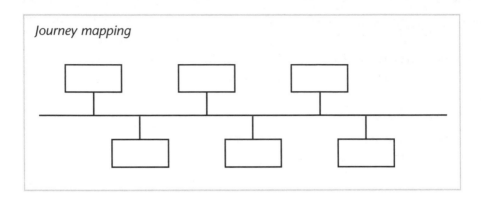

Journey mapping

Drawing pictures

Some children may need to draw pictures to support story planning, for example, four or six pictures to outline the main events. The details in each picture can help some children to understand the relationship between the main ideas (what each picture is broadly about) and the supporting details (what each picture includes).

The questions approach

Identifying the 'who, what, how, where and when' of a story or other text is another good way to anchor thoughts.

The above suggestions remind us that there are two distinct levels of planning, the second following on from the first. Children need to be taught how to plan in order to generate ideas and to organise the ideas that have been generated. They need to know the purpose in order to select the most appropriate planning strategy. Perhaps the spider diagram is best for generating ideas, while the flowchart can be used to organise the ideas into a sequential order.

A final thought on planning comes from Sharples (1999):

> A written plan or outline is an expression of the *'writer then'* . . . as the writing progresses, the plan becomes increasingly out of step with the *'writer now'* and needs to be reinterpreted to fit the changing situation.

Of course, this refers to longer pieces of work, but the principle is sound and applies to children too. A plan should not be a straitjacket to stifle the creativity of the writing. The thinking should still be going on until the final word of the last line of a piece of text has been written.

Redrafting and editing writing

Right! So we've finished the first draft of our story, play, poem or account of the school trip. There's nothing more to be done. We can now place it on the wall or wherever else as 'done'. Wrong! If the piece of writing is for an intended readership, the redrafting is as important as the first draft. Consider the NLS objective that refers to redrafting: to review and edit writing to produce a final form matched to the needs of an identified reader (Y5, T2).

Throughout Key Stage 2, the emphasis is firmly on polishing writing for an intended readership. As writers become more competent they should aim to write like readers. This is not to suggest that all writing needs to be redrafted and intensively processed for presentation. We don't want to de-motivate learners by making writing too laborious. So let's take a look at the redrafting and editing process for those pieces for which it is merited.

What is the difference between redrafting and editing? By redrafting I am referring to the process of looking at the whole piece in terms of:

- The overall shape – its beginning, middle and end.
- The structure – are the paragraphs linked into each other so that the writing flows?
- Is there a clear sequence of events?
- If non-fiction, is the format right for this particular piece?
- Does the choice of first or third person work best for this particular piece?
- Is the tone and style suitable for the readership and the type of piece? For example, informal and chatty using community language, or formal using carefully constructed Standard English.

It is important to view the whole piece before looking in detail at its component parts.

By editing, I am referring to the finer details in terms of:

- Sentence structure – is the word order OK?
- Grammar – is it correct in terms of verb tenses and word classes?
- Vocabulary – are the words varied and right for the particular piece?
- Punctuation – does it work within the text to create the right impact?

Children could draw up a simple checklist to help with the editing process.

The editing checklist

My sentences:

1   Does each sentence make sense?
2   Does each word follow on from the last – in the right order?
3   Do all my verbs match each other – past/present/future?
4   Have I put a full stop or a question mark at the end of each sentence?
5   Have I put a capital letter at the start of each sentence?

My choice of words:

6   Are my nouns colourful enough?
7   Are my verbs strong?
8   Have I used too many adjectives and adverbs?
9   Do my main meaning-carrying words really express what I want to say?

My spellings:

10 Are the tricky words correct?
11 Are the other spellings as good as I can make them?

Children could go through their checklist and look at each aspect of the writing either by themselves or in pairs. It is important to differentiate the editing process for different groups. Some may need to be taught how to look at the trees (details) within the wood (whole text). Conversely, others may not be able to see the wood for the trees.

The editing of the spelling may be particularly problematic. Some children will be able to use a wordbook to look up the tricky words. When spelling unknown words, if children have been encouraged to hear sounds within words and can identify these in the right order, they could be taught to say the word they have written and ask themselves if all the sounds they hear in the word are there on the page. Can they hear any other sounds? Of course, children who can use a dictionary should be encouraged to use one independently.

The process of redrafting and editing is intended to develop independent writing, but the process must also be manageable and fun. Try:

- Letting children work in pairs or small groups for mutual support and to encourage critical analysis of each other's work – talk is valuable.

- Presenting the task in bite-sized chunks rather than the whole lot at once.

- Analysing the work only in accordance with the writing objectives for that lesson or week – for example, is 'spelling' or 'sentence structure' the focus of today?

- Using colourful markers, highlighters and other editing tools – much less boring than pencils.

- Only bothering with the redrafting and editing when it matters!

Go for quality rather than quantity. Children will then be encouraged to take pride in their work and realise that a few pieces of good writing are better than many pieces of unfinished or poor examples.

A final point. Not all pieces of writing need to be presented as a final copy – part of the value of the redrafting/editing process lies in the act itself, especially when time is short. For some children, the act of re-copying the final copy is the de-motivator. Be sensitive to the links between process and product.

Dealing with difficulties

I am lucky. I can enjoy writing without any problems getting in the way of my pleasure. Perhaps you too are one of those people for whom writing is easy, and, to some extent, pleasurable and free from anxiety. Let's consider why some learners struggle and how we might alleviate their difficulties.

Reluctance to write

Why are children reluctant to write? The source could be one or some of the following:

- handwriting problems;
- spelling problems;
- no imagination;
- not interested;
- can't see the purpose.

Once we have identified the source of the problem, we are in a better position to address it. If children can't see the purpose of the activity, then give them a real purpose. Who is going to read their piece? Why? What will happen to their piece when it is written?

If those learners, who we know *can* write, appear not interested, has there been enough discussion to provide a stimulus for their ideas? Have they been offered some choice? Are the reluctant writers mainly boys? If so, perhaps we can tempt them by linking writing with topics in which they may be interested. For example:

- Football or sport – a poster to advertise a new strip, a news report on the game, a recount of the match from the point of view of one of the players and so on.
- Younger children could bring in toys of their own to stimulate both fiction and non-fiction writing.
- Links with topical films or TV programmes.

As the saying goes, 'we can take the horse to water but we can't make it drink'. With regard to writing, we can provide water that is as fresh, sweet and inviting as possible.

Handwriting and spelling problems

If children have significant handwriting or spelling problems, these must be addressed for the writing to develop. Could children who struggle with handwriting or letter formation write directly onto a word processor sometimes? Alternatively, could such children have a scribe for part of the work? While scribing for children is not recommended, in cases where children are genuinely overwhelmed by the size of the task, sharing the writing itself (not necessarily the thinking and the planning) could help.

In certain circumstances, children could try working with word cards as a release from pencil and paper. A child could tell you what he/she wants to write. You write the words (or some of them) onto cards for the child to sequence into the right order and stick into the writing book. While I acknowledge that these strategies don't get to the heart of the difficulty, they may enable more children with handwriting problems to experience some success in the compositional aspects of writing. For a small proportion of learners, writing with pencil or pen onto paper is simply a long-term problem that will not go away.

For those with poor spelling you could try:

- The magic line – when the spelling of a particular word threatens to halt the writing process, encourage children to put a line accompanied by the initial letter of the word, or any letters a child thinks may be in the word, with the intention to return to that word later. Nothing is worse than agonising over a word and losing the writing momentum.

- Writing the word on a scrap of paper for the child to use the LSCWC method of writing it down.

- Reminding children that the writing is more important than the spellings, when it really is, to encourage children to 'have a go' at the spellings.

- Responding to writing in process without reference to spellings, only to the sentence or the text structure.

- Operate a 'buddy' system, for spellings – a child can ask an assigned peer for help with some of the more difficult spellings.

- Providing a suitable dictionary for those who can use it quickly and independently.

- Providing a word mat for the most common tricky words that are likely to be needed.

Writing collaboratively is also helpful for all children who struggle with writing, whether for ideas or with the secretarial aspects of the task.

Language limitations

This is a difficult problem as language limitations affect every aspect of writing. Often children use the same words over and over again (*nice, good, big*), either because they can't think of any others, or because they can't spell the word they have thought of, and decide to be 'safe' rather than take risks. These children struggle to include adventurous words in their writing and the content may lack the vitality that comes from using a variety of vocabulary in a range of ways. They cannot write for effect!

Nevertheless, we can actively seek to develop vocabulary and language structure as part of our general support. In addition, for those children whose language limitations seriously affect their writing ability, you could:

● Draw out from the child what vocabulary he can provide, then add to it to increase his vocabulary choices.

● If time is short, provide specific vocabulary for children to choose from – for example, words that promote emotions of fear for a story, or words to describe a person or animal (discuss meanings to ensure understanding).

● Provide models of sentences – statements, questions, instructions.

● Provide some useful phrases or sentence starters for the child to use.

● Provide sentences with words or phrases missing for the child to insert – to alleviate sentence structure difficulties.

● Provide a writing frame for structuring text level writing.

It is difficult to enable children with language limitations to find success in writing as we are attempting to develop the language, as well as enhance the writing as we go along. Try to think what aspects of language in particular children need help with and adapt some of the suggestions above to the problem. For example, if a child does not use pronouns in speech, provide some and discuss with the child (as part of the redrafting process) how they can be used.

'I don't know what to write'

We have all come across the child who sits with pen in hand and simply can't bring any ideas to mind. This may be because:

- The initial discussion and planning has not provided sufficient stimulus (the brain has not been stimulated and activated).
- The child needs a visual stimulus – for example, objects or pictures.
- The child is not interested in the topic and needs some further choices.
- The child is not fully aware of the nature of the task itself and therefore cannot dredge up ideas for something that is not clear in his/her mind.
- The child is a social learner and is stimulated more by collaborative writing.

Clearly, such children can't write with others all of the time or we would never find out what they can do for themselves, but a balance of the above strategies used some of the time may help.

Run out of steam but no structure?

What about the child who sets off and covers half a page in the first five minutes? All the ideas tumble out in no coherent order and the writing is then regarded as 'done'. The child has quite literally run out of steam. The ideas have not resulted in an understandable text level piece, but the child has nothing more to say – it is all there on the page. Such a writer needs to regain pace and control. You could encourage the child to:

- Plan more carefully and stick to the plan by using pictures or key words to fix each part of the writing in the mind.
- Read each paragraph once it is written to check if each sentence matches the main idea.
- Highlight the key sentences in each paragraph to maintain in the mind a skeleton outline of the text.
- Slow down and try not to put all the ideas down on paper at once.
- Perceive writing at text level as something that needs time.

The problem here lies in the planning and later, in the redrafting, as this learner needs to structure writing and prevent ideas from running out of control.

Writes short, stilted sentences?

You surely recognise this one. A child writes in staccato-type sentences with little variation of structure. Listen to how the child speaks – the child who writes short sentences may well speak in short sentences. You may need to:

- Provide a range of different sentence starters to encourage some variation.
- Model different sentence structures.
- Teach the child how to use conjunctions in speech and in writing.

Writes long, rambling sentences that get lost?

Again, listen to the speech. Many children speak with no pauses and the ideas flood out with no structure or sequence to them. They will try to tell you their news, but this comes out as a jumble of disconnected information. This rambling will be reflected in the writing. On the one hand, there needs to be a grip, but we don't want to inhibit children's flow of ideas by continually putting on the brakes. Rambling sentence writers do need to:

- Check themselves sentences to tease out the main idea of each and to ask where the full stop, question marks, commas and so on should go.
- Focus on the purpose of punctuation within and between sentences.
- Focus on meaning through rereading in order to make sense of sentences.
- Look at examples of short sentences to see where these might fit their own writing as part of the redrafting process.
- During the redrafting process, actively search for sentences that can be split.

Ramblers are rarely short of ideas – the problem is getting the ideas down with due regard to sentence structure and punctuation.

Children for whom English is an additional language (EAL)

The strategies for helping children with EAL are no different than those for most children who experience difficulties. Many of the strategies listed above will support these groups. The sample of writing (see below) was written by a child with Russian as his first language, and illustrates the problems in spelling and writing that arise partly from difficulties in acquiring spoken English.

Encouraging EAL children to write in their first language if they are able will also help to maintain their flow of ideas when composition is the main objective. They can then tell you what they have written and, if time allows, this can be written into English.

One Christmas I felt happy. At Christmas I go with my Dad to a park. There is a field... lot of snowing. Then we go home. I felt really and really happy. Then is night time. I go upstairs. Then I go fast asleep. When I woke up I go downstairs then. Then Christmas tree is present. I got a 'Buzz Light Year'. I so happy. Then I start play with Buzz. I really wanted Buzz.

Interactive writing

The focused writing session can detract from its nature as 'all encompassing'. Hall (1999) has some excellent ideas for making writing purposeful, real and 'interactive' with a response element that is rarely apparent when writing is limited to the literacy hour. Hall describes interactive writing as 'two people writing to each other for an extended period of time'. Arising from this, we get the relationship between reader and writer that is the essence of writing. The two people could be:

● Teacher or teaching assistant and child.

● Two children in the same class.

● Two children in different classes.

Palmer (2002) reiterates one of my main principles: 'Moving from skills to thrills – fun, motivation, stimulation, the stuff that leads children to learn, not just slog.' We need to think deeply about those two key phrases 'from skills to thrills' and 'not just slog'. The NLS objectives lead most of the work on writing, but simply trawling through these does tend to neglect the 'thrills' of writing.

If the aim is to enable most children to become independent writers then the message is clear: encourage children to want to write and make it *real*.

Summary

In this chapter I have looked at:

● The main points for sharing and guiding writing.
● Planning what to write.
● Redrafting and editing.
● How to deal with significant difficulties.

Chapter 8

Supporting the assessment and monitoring process

Assessing and recording play an integral role in the teaching and learning process. This chapter considers:

- Assessing children's writing.
- How children can assess their own writing.
- Monitoring writing progress.
- Involving parents in assessing writing.
- Recording information for reviews and reports.

■ Supporting the assessment of children's writing

How can teaching assistants support the assessment of children's work and do justice to the efforts made by learners and adults? *Removing Barriers to Achievement* (DfES 2004) emphasises 'assessment for learning'. This means that assessment should influence the teaching, supporting and ultimately the learning that takes place in classrooms. Assessment for learning implies that we assess the *processes* as well as the *products*.

To assess the writing process, we need to look at what children are doing during the planning, the writing task itself and redrafting. Evidence can stem from:

- Writing in different subject areas.
- Writing alone.
- Collaborating with others.

We can also, as part of the assessment of process:

- Read children's writing logs (see later).
- Talk to children about their writing.
- Appraise writing 'as it is being done'.
- Hold writing conferences (see later).
- Organise writing 'surgeries' for problem-solving in groups.

The criteria we use to assess completed pieces of writing could include the following.

At text level (fiction and non-fiction)

- The coherence of the text – clear paragraphs, good use of connectives.
- The content – interest, suitable tone.
- Clarity of genre (text type) – can be clearly identified as a story, poem, play or (if non-fiction) a recount, report, instructional, persuasive, discursive or explanatory text.
- Fitness for intended audience – style, level of formality.
- Format (if non-fiction) – use of bullets, boxes and other signposts.
- Use of diagrams (non-fiction).

At sentence level

- Variations in type – statements, questions, instructions, exclamations.
- Balance of different sentence lengths.
- Use of clauses within sentences.
- Use of grammar – Standard English or community language.

At word level

- Balance of short and longer words.
- Use of adventurous vocabulary – to promote interest for the reader.
- Suitability of vocabulary for its intended audience.

● How the vocabulary is used for effect.

Chapter 3 explored the P scales together with the National Curriculum level descriptions. While some summative assessment may be linked to a National Curriculum level, criterion-referenced checklists, such as the one above, focus on the skills learners need to improve.

Giving feedback to children

If the purpose is to motivate and to move children onto the next level, feedback needs to:

● Be clear and precise – what is good, what needs to be improved.

● Be given as the writing is being done or as soon as the writing is finished (to maintain momentum).

● Indicate the next steps – at word, sentence and text levels.

Children self-assessing writing

There are many reasons why children need to contribute to their own assessment process. We all agree, but how do we manage it? I have found the following strategies useful.

Writing log

Children spontaneously enter into a diary or exercise book their thoughts about writing and evaluations of their own progress. Over time, the entries constitute an interesting account of writing from the perspective of the learners. I have found some sad comments in writing logs, for example, 'I hate writing'. But such honest negativity can become a positive strategy for resolving problems. At least you know what they are thinking. The log also provides a stimulus for a writing conference.

Extract from a child's writing log	
Date	Comments
13.5.04	Did a poem on 'My family' today – good that we don't have to do sentences. Don't want to be a poet.
29.5.04	I wish I could write better letters – my writing is so untidy.
10.6.04	Been on school trip today – we always have to write about it. Mrs Benson showed me how to make notes to help me not to forget what we did.

Writing conference

This is a progress interview between the child and an adult (teaching assistants often have the opportunity to do this). We might do this once per term, or half-year or more frequently. All children can talk about their writing progress at a level that is right for them.

Teaching assistant's notes from a child's writing conference	
Name: John Average	Date: 13.6.04
Compared John's story 'The flying cat' with the one last term on 'My Gran's a witch'. We both agreed that he is using more colourful vocabulary (he highlighted this himself), writing longer sentences with better use of conjunctions, and he is experimenting with different kinds of diagrams in his non-fiction writing. John would like to do more of this as he enjoys non-fiction writing. He says he struggles to find ideas for writing stories.	

Group-based surgeries

Children are offered regular opportunities to talk with an adult about writing with the focus on problem-solving. Such talk can be illuminating. Children may tell you that they struggle with long sentences, don't understand paragraphs, or feel that their writing is just 'not good'.

Notes from a group surgery	
Date	Comments on discussions – Group 3
24.1.04	Jasmine and Betty said they didn't understand the passive tense – must have a group session on this.
29.1.04	Talked with Paul and John about poetry – said they hated it. We drew up some topics they were interested in for next time – space, cars, football.
3.2.04	Lucy, Peter and Elise – main problem is punctuation and sentence structure.

Making children aware of what they are learning

It is amazing how many children try to engage in the learning process without understanding what they are meant to be learning. If we want to encourage children to take responsibility for their learning, then they must understand their objectives and targets.

The child's own self-assessment checklist

Based on the criteria above, a child's checklist prompts self-evaluation. There is great value in pairs of children evaluating (sensitively) each other's writing. But children need to know precisely what they are looking for when redrafting, so the checklist needs to be clear and precise. The example list below illustrates possible questions that might prompt children to evaluate their writing at word, sentence and text levels. Such a checklist could be adapted to suit different attainment levels. If laminated, they could become **writing mats**.

Child's own writing checklist
My own writing checklist:
● Are my nouns and verbs strong?
● Have I used too many adjectives or adverbs?
● Have I overused some words?

- Do my sentences make sense?
- Have I put full stops at the end of my sentences?
- Have I put capital letters at the beginning?
- Do my sentences have different beginnings?
- Do I have some long and some short sentences?
- Do my paragraphs stick to one main idea?
- Does my writing have a clear beginning, middle and end?
- Which genre does my text fit into? Does it fit the model I have been working from?

Comparing children's writing 'then and now'

Part of the self-assessment process involves children comparing writing from last year or term with 'now'. Children often find it difficult to talk beyond the generalities of writing progress. They will say that their writing is 'good' or 'better', but when you ask them how it is good or better, there is no response.

We need to involve children in analysing writing in detail otherwise how can they know what aspects to develop? Try to encourage children to look critically at their own pieces. This will be helped by the sensitive asking of questions such as those in the checklist above to help focus the discussion.

Highlighting is always a useful means of identifying differences between 'then' and 'now', for example, we might highlight the more extensive use of multi-clause sentences, the spelling of more high-frequency words, or the more adventurous vocabulary. Try to find *something* (however small a step) to illustrate progress. Most children are making some progress, however minimal, and deserve to have this identified and their efforts celebrated. It may be difficult for some children with learning difficulties, and their parents, to appreciate progress unless we draw their attention to the small steps.

Remember – think in details, not generalities.

Monitoring writing progress

Monitoring compares achievement with potential. For children with an **IEP**, a review meeting would be the forum for monitoring progress. Monitoring is an essential follow-up to assessment – without the monitoring of progress, there is no point to the assessment. We need to look carefully at the assessment information we have collated and analyse it in terms of progress. How do we know if a child is making sufficient progress in writing? Consider the following three children:

- Lucy (Year 2) has severe learning difficulties. She has achieved National Curriculum Level P7 for writing. Reasonable progress for Lucy would be to attain one P level each year. To expect Lucy to 'catch up' with her peers would be unrealistic, but we do need to mark the small steps of progress and check that they are in line with reasonably high expectations for Lucy.
- Michael (Year 3) attained Level 2 in the National Curriculum assessment tests. Michael would be expected to achieve in line with the average for his year group.
- Bethany (Year 6) attained Level 3 in the Key Stage 1 National Curriculum assessment tests and has demonstrated above-average ability in writing all through primary school. She should achieve well beyond the average Level 4 in the Key Stage 2 National Curriculum assessments.

If children are not making progress at the expected rates, then we need to question why. The whole point of monitoring is to look at the rate of progress year on year, or term by term, and ask questions about individual learners. Only by *knowing children as learners* can we have reasonable expectations for individuals.

What if some learners are not progressing according to expectations? Is the problem outside of school or does the learning environment lack something for that particular learner? With regard to the National Curriculum inclusion statements, and our support for writing, we might ask:

- Are the challenges right for that child?
- Has there been access to the learning opportunities?
- Has this child's particular learning needs been addressed?

The assessment and monitoring processes need to go hand in hand if they are to inform teaching, supporting and learning.

Recording information for reviews and reports

So, having observed children writing in many different situations, how could we record our observations? See the example below. You might wish to look at the comments and decide which reflect the writing process and which stem from having analysed the final product.

Example of individual assessment record from observations		
Date	Subject	Skills and achievements observed
16.1.04	Science	Used writing frame to work independently on report.
19.1.04	History	Wrote newspaper article on invention of Spinning Jenny – good use of passive tense.
23.1.04	Art	Wrote own page on Van Gogh (as contribution to class book on famous artists).
26.1.04	Literacy hour	Noted good range of sentence lengths from piece on 'Sharks' – constructs two-clause sentences, using basic conjunctions.
28.1.04	Geography	Designed matrix for advantages and disadvantages of living in hot and cold countries – demonstrated good awareness of 'comparison' as way of thinking.

Below is an example of how we might record collaborative work on writing.

Recording collaborative work on writing	
Date	Half/term – Jan/Feb 2004
12.1.04	Jamie contributed to the group spider diagram for a story.
15.1.04	Anne edited Jane's writing and suggested more colourful vocabulary.
22.1.04	Anne/Jane worked well together – splitting Anne's long sentences.
11.2.04	Jamie/Peter changed all the verb tenses from present to past.
16.2.04	Peter still struggled to join in the judging of the best poem.

What do we do with the records?

The bulk of records are in the form of notes made on a daily or weekly basis. They should include:

- The writing skills worked on with dates.
- How individual children have responded.
- The skills and knowledge you have observed.

Whether you record on a form designed for the purpose or in an exercise book is less important than the quality of the notes made. These need to be significant in terms of learning, and reflect the objectives or targets that children are working on.

Over time, these continual notes build up into a huge file and it is difficult to cope with the growing volume. Yet, unless we use some of the information positively, what has been the point of recording? For children with an IEP, the ongoing notes may need to be summarised into a cumulative report required by the SENCO. I would find it useful to summarise on a regular basis the *main staging points of learning* for children supported as a contribution to the overall monitoring process.

I often find it sad when teaching assistants tell me that the records they maintain are rarely read or used by anyone other than themselves, yet they can make a valuable contribution as part of the assessment and monitoring team. If your school maintains an assessment file for individual learners, the following information on writing might be included:

- A termly summary of the teaching assistant's observational notes.
- Children's writing logs.
- Notes on the child's writing conference.
- Examples of writing over time to show the 'then' and 'now'.

Such cumulative records would build up into a manageable record of progress over a longer period of time, for example, to show a child's rate of progress summatively over a year or a key stage.

Involving parents in assessing writing

Parents can only be involved if they have some awareness of how writing is taught in school. Many teaching assistants talk to parents at either end of the school day, offering valuable opportunities to communicate information on writing. Without overburdening parents, and checking that this is in accordance with school policy, you could:

- Comment (in simple terms) on the class objectives for writing this term.
- Inform parents of one or two main targets their child is working on and invite their support for these.
- Show parents copies of their child's writing and point out the progress features (in the child's hearing where possible).
- Give parents, through this informal talk process, some of your acquired tips on responding to children's writing – for example, finding something good before pointing out errors.

Summary

In this chapter I have looked at:

- The type of assessments, monitoring and recording that informs teaching and support work, and enhances learning.
- Self-assessment as the pivot around which assessment works for all learners.
- How assessment needs to focus on what children can do and to move them on rather than dwelling on what they fail to achieve.
- How assessment *for* learning needs to reflect the cross-curricular and ongoing characteristics *of* learning.

Conclusion

The aim of this book has been to guide readers through the processes of children becoming competent and independent writers. Although the focus has been on composition, it is recognised that spelling and handwriting also play a supporting role in the development of independent writing.

Many children struggle with writing and an implicit thread throughout the book has been the expectation that schools will track back to earlier objectives so that all learners are set realistic challenges that enable achievement. I hope that this book helps to facilitate that process. I find it sad that many children never reach the level of competence needed to communicate effectively through writing, and to enjoy it.

Whether you are an inexperienced teaching assistant or whether you are one of the many higher-level teaching assistants with enhanced responsibility for children's achievements, I hope that the information, practical suggestions and advice have met your needs. I hope also that your support of children's writing is enriched through having read and absorbed the content of this book.

References

Adams, J. (2004) *Developing Emotional Literacy in Schools*. Corby: First and Best in Education Ltd.

ATL (2004) *Emotional Literacy Update*, Issue 5. London: Optimus Publishing.

Bayley, R. and Day, S. (2003) *Supporting Children's Writing Development in the Early Years*. Walsall: Lawrence Educational Publications.

DfEE/QCA (1999) *The National Curriculum: Handbook for Primary Teachers in England*. London: DfEE/QCA.

DfEE/QCA (2000) *Curriculum Guidance for the Foundation Stage*. London: DfEE/QCA.

DfES (2001) *Developing Early Writing*. London: DfES.

DfES (2004) *Removing Barriers to Achievement*. London: DfES.

Gorman, T. and Brooks, G. (1996) *Assessing Young Children's Writing*. London: Basic Skills Agency.

Hall, N. (1999) *Interactive Writing in the Primary School*. Reading: Reading and Language Information Centre.

National Literacy Strategy (2001) *National Literacy Strategy Framework for Teaching*. London: DfES.

Palmer, S. (2002) 'From skills to thrills', *TES Teacher*, 15 November.

QCA (2001) *Supporting the Target Setting Process*, revised version. London: QCA.

Sharples, M. (1999) *How We Write*. London: Routledge.

Wray, D. (2002) *Practical Ways to Teach Writing*. Reading: Reading and Language Information Centre.

Resources

Writing work often happens with nothing more than pencil and paper, but there is a wealth of materials now available that help to bring life to writing and support the busy adult. No purchased resource can replace a skilled and sensitive adult as the number one resource for writing, but the following list offers ideas to support adults and learners. The list indicates the range of materials available to support writing. While many of the resources are interactive and stimulating for pupils to use with an adult, or independently, I recognise the occasional need for worksheets as practice materials so these are also included.

General materials

We can get by with very little: different coloured paper, pencils and pens, markers and other writing tools, for example, white boards, can help to support motivation. A range of objects and pictures provides stimulation and ideas for writing, and a collection of text types will also come in handy when models are needed. If time is available, games such as bingo, snap, dominoes can be made cheaply in a few minutes by having coloured card to hand, although there are many games available to purchase.

For reference

A range of dictionaries and thesauruses are needed if colourful vocabulary is the aim. Try the *Word Whiz* from Kingscourt or the *Collins Compact Thesaurus: The Ultimate Wordfinder* (for pupils who can read fluently).

Materials for focused sentence work

Learning Materials Ltd

These comprise simple materials for children who need catch-up practice in writing:

- *Writing Sentences* (photocopiable), early KS1.
- *Support for Basic Grammar* – Books 1–8 (photocopiable), covers KS1 and KS2 work.
- *Cloze Pegs* – focuses on meaning within sentences (photocopiable), early KS2.
- *New Cloze* – contains two differentiated levels of text for each passage (photocopiable).
- *Writing for a Purpose* – intended as practice or homework materials (photocopiable).

Easylearn

- *Stop it!* – grammar and punctuation work (photocopiable), KS1.
- *Stop it, Editor!* – full of texts to be corrected (photocopiable), KS2.

Smart Kids

- *Action Bingo* – focus on verbs at work, interactive.
- *Verbs at Work* – magnetic grammar game, deals with verb tenses, interactive.
- Magnetic sentence building sets – upper KS1 and KS2, interactive.
- Vocabulary work – on synonyms, homonyms, antonyms (opposites), interactive

LDA

- *Brickworks* – for sentence building at KS1, interactive.
- *Grammar through the Literacy Hour* – big books for Years 3 and 4.

Philip & Tacey

- The grammar games: *Odd One Out, What's That, Then? All Change, What's Wrong?* The four categories cover sentence level work for KS2 – this is an interactive game for groups that is self-checking.
- Sentence completion game, halves of sentences to match up – interactive activity for children who have covered the phonic work at KS1 (up to vowel digraph level).
- *Silly Sensible* – focuses on meaning. All sentences are grammatically correct, but only half make logical sense; interactive and fun activity for KS1 and early KS2.

ICT support for writing

ICT can develop writing skills as well as the ICT skills per se, and often provides the motivation that some children need to keep going. Your school could check out the Clicker range of programmes from SEMERC.

- *Clicker 4* is *the* resource for supporting learner writers at all levels (from Crick Software Ltd). *Word Bar* and *Text Ease* are also useful additions, as is *Cloze-Pro. Clicker Animations* support young writers by moving pictures, graphics and sound.
- *Ready for Writing* is an introductory word processor that uses talking words and pictures to stimulate early writing (from REM).
- *Texthelp* – a new resource for struggling writers that offers 'talk support' (from Texthelp Systems).

Ideas and further reading for the adults

- Additional Literacy Support Materials – four modules originally designed as early KS2 booster work, contain ideas and games for catch-up work (DfEE 1999).
- *Storylines* – an anthology of 50 ideas for using large puppets, dolls and soft toys, staff working in Early Years settings (from Lawrence Educational Publications).

- *Let's Write* – starting points for writing experiences; also support early writing (from Lawrence Educational Publications).

- *Writing Models*: for KS2 year groups (available from David Fulton Publishers).

- *How to Teach Story Writing at KS1* and *How to Teach Poetry Writing at KS1* (available from David Fulton Publishers).

- *How to Teach Fiction Writing at KS2* and *How to Teach Poetry Writing at KS2* (available from David Fulton Publishers).

- *Poetry In and Out of the Literacy Hour* is published by the University of Reading.

- *Developing Early Writing* (DfEE 2001) also contains ideas and 'how to' advice.

Useful addresses

Crick Software Ltd, Crick House, Boarden Close, Moulton Park, Northampton NN3 6LF. Tel: 01604 671691; Fax: 01604 671692; www.cricksoft.com.

Easylearn Ltd, Trent House, Fiskerton, Southwell, Notts NG25 0UH. Tel: 01636 830240; Fax: 01636 830162; www.easylearn.co.uk.

Kingscourt/McGraw Hill, Shoppenhangers Road, Maidenhead, Berks SL6 2BT. Tel: 0800 317457; Fax: 0870 241 6398; www.mcgraw-hill.co.uk.

Lawrence Educational Publications, 17 Redruth Road, Walsall, West Midlands WS5 3EJ. Tel/fax: 01922 643833.

LDA, Duke Street, Wisbech, Cambs PE13 2AE. Tel: 01945 463441; www.LDAlearning.com.

Learning Materials Ltd, Dixon Street, Wolverhampton, West Midlands WV2 2BX. Tel: 01902 454026; Fax: 01902 457596; www.learningmaterials.co.uk.

Philip & Tacey Ltd, North Way, Andover, Hants SP10 5BA. Tel: 01264 332171; Fax: 01264 384808; www.philipandtacey.co.uk.

REM, Freepost, TU823, Great Western House, Langport, Somerset TA10 9YU. Tel: 01458 254700; Fax: 01458 254701; www.r-e-m.co.uk.

SEMERC, Granada Learning, Granada Television, Quay Street, Manchester M60 9EA. Tel: 0161 827 2927; Fax: 0161 827 2966; www.semerc.com.

Smart Kids (UK) Ltd, 5 Station Road, Hungerford, Berkshire RG17 0DY. Tel: 01488 644644; Fax: 01488 644645; www.smartkids.co.uk.

Texthelp Systems Ltd, Enkalon Business Centre, 25 Randalstown Road, Antrim, N. Ireland BT41 4LJ. Tel: 0800 328 7910.

Glossary

Active verb	Form of verb structure that follows after the subject of the sentence, e.g. he *fell* in the mud, she *was running* around the park, the children *laughed* at the dog. Most of the verbs we use in everyday speech are active.
Adjective	Usually, words that describe nouns, e.g. *brown* fox, *blue* sky, *tall* man, *falling* tree, *cruel* eyes.
Adverb	Usually, words that describe verbs, e.g. ran *quickly*, ate *slowly*.
Barrier	Something that prevents access to the curriculum and gets in the way of progress.
Blurb	The persuasive text at the front or back of a book designed to 'sell' it to the reader.
Clauses	Groups of words that fit together grammatically to express an idea and can be combined into a sentence. One sentence may contain a number of clauses.
Complex sentence	Has two or more clauses.
Conflict	Tension within fiction that arises from different characters having opposing goals and aspirations.
Conjunction	Word used to join simple sentences together, e.g. *because, and, but, when, if, as, so*.
Determiners	The little words that have minimal meaning per se. They are not meaning-carrying words, but they add precision to the sentence in terms of meaning and contribute to grammatically complete language, e.g. *an, my, he, what, said, want*.

Direct speech	The exact words said in dialogue that should be placed between speech marks within a sentence, e.g. "Go away", "Buzz off", "Come here", "Get me that book from the shelf".
Dominant sound	The strongest sound in a word, the one we are most likely to detect as the word is spoken.
Emergent writing	Writing that develops at the child's own pace, that is nurtured and guided so that it emerges naturally through a trial and error approach to learning.
Fiction	Texts written from the imagination, not from true facts.
Format	How a text is set out on the page in different ways.
Genre	Refers to the type of text, e.g. novel, historical, crime, contemporary, report, persuasion text, recount.
Grammar	The structural rules of a language, they govern Standard English.
High-frequency words	Those listed in the NLS Framework for Teaching as the ones we read and write most often, *see also* Tricky words.
IEP review	Meeting to review progress for children who have an individual education plan, usually held each term.
Inflectional ending	Ending that may change the tense, number, gender or case of the word, but does not change its word class, e.g. *ing, es, s, ed* as in chang*ing*, bus*es*, cat*s* and pott*ed*.
LSCWC	Look, Say, Cover, Write, Check – strategy for learning how to spell words visually.
Metaphor	Describes an object or action using a word or phrase from the imagination, not literal, e.g. a dirty trick, a tall tale, the Green Party (in politics) – a surprisingly large part of our speech is metaphorical.
Monitoring	Evaluation of progress over time.
Narrative links	Words or phrases that support the coherence of paragraphs and chapters by referring back to something stated earlier, e.g. as *mentioned previously, he,*

	they (most pronouns refer to a noun further back in the text), *as he recalled from the last occasion.*
Non-fiction	Texts comprising true facts.
Noun	Concrete nouns are often naming words, e.g. *table, man, lamp, eggs.* Some nouns can be more abstract, e.g. *mediocrity, coarseness, enchantment.* Usually, the subject or object of the sentence – the *dog* bit the *man.* Nouns can be singular or plural – *bus, buses, cat, cats.*
Object (of the sentence)	Person or thing to which the subject does something, e.g. the man threw *the ball,* or in passive, *the ball* was thrown by the man.
Orientation	The way in which a letter must always be written to remain *that same* letter, e.g. the letters 'b, d and p' are the same shape but are different letters because of their constant orientation.
Passive verb	Formal form of verb structure with the object placed before it, e.g. books *were read,* plates *were thrown,* evidence *was collected.*
Phonological awareness	Understanding of the relationship between how words sound and how they are spelt.
Plot	The storyline, the sequence of events that make up a work of fiction.
Prepositions	Words that describe where things are, e.g. *under, over, on, away, beyond, beneath, at.*
Pronoun	Word used in place of a noun that refers back to a noun in the text, e.g. *he, they, which, who, she.*
Reflexive verbs	Verbs that have the subject as the object, e.g. we wash ourselves, dress ourselves.
Relative clauses	These often support or refer back to an earlier noun phrase, and often start with *who, whom, whose, which, that.* The man, *who was walking his dog at the time,* saw the robbery. The thieves, *whose attention was diverted elsewhere,* did not see the police car arrive. A relative clause cannot stand alone as a sentence.

Reported (often known as indirect) **speech**	This describes what someone says without using the exact words of the dialogue, e.g. the man told her to go away, she asked him to get her red book.
Root word	Main part of a multi-syllabic word from which extended words with the same meaning are formed, or extended words with different meanings are derived, e.g. *graph* as in graphical, graphics, autograph, biographical.
Simile	Figure of speech used openly to compare, often uses the word 'as', e.g. as red as fire, as white as snow, as heavy as lead.
Subject	The who or what of the sentence, e.g. *The man* threw the ball, *He* was angry.
Synopsis	Summary or outline of a text.
Syntax	Grammatical arrangement of words in sentences.
Text	Any type of writing that combines words and sentences, fiction or non-fiction.
Theme	What the text is mainly about, e.g. greed, jealousy, possessiveness, money, getting what you want from life – describes the essence of the text.
Tricky words	Words that are not phonically regular (as referred to in the NLS), do not sound as they are spelled, e.g. *come, said, go, my, should,* and must be learned visually.
Verb pattern/ structure	Verbs made up of more than one word, e.g. *was running, have been eating, were* due *to go, would have gone.*
Word class	Grouping of words that broadly share the same syntactical characteristics in sentences, e.g. as nouns, verbs, adverbs etc.
Word form	Different forms of words derived from the same root by adding prefixes and suffixes, e.g. chant, chant*ed*, chant*ing*, *en*chant*ment*, *disen*chant*ed*.
Writing frame	Structured support that provides a scaffold for writing.

Writing mat Card with important facts on it that can be laminated and placed constantly on the child's desk for reference when writing.

Index